PRACTICAL ASSESSMENTS
for Literature-Based Reading Classrooms

BY ADELE FIDERER

SCHOLASTIC
PROFESSIONAL BOOKS

New York • Toronto • London • Auckland • Sydney

 Acknowledgments

I would like to thank the many people whose work and contributions have made this book possible. I owe a special debt to two of my teacher-researcher colleagues. Lila Berger provided assessments, children's work products, and her knowledge of second-grade readers. Lila also assisted me with various chores in preparing this manuscript for the publisher. In addition, first-grade classroom vignettes and examples of young children's literary thinking came from studies conducted by Mary Hayter.

Marian Absgarten, Ellen Anders, Ethel Huttar, Ann Newbury, and Valerie Rein classroom tested some of the various assessment strategies and tools that appear in this book, and they shared their insights with me. Additional assessment tools, samples of students' work, and suggestions for strengthening the home-school connection were contributed by Bill Ackerman, Judy Grosz, Barbara Jansz, Barbara MacMahon, Heidi Menzel, Margaret O'Farrell, and Joelle Weiss. I will always be especially grateful to my own students who showed me what worked and did not work in our assessment processes.

A special thanks to Beebe Allyson Garcia, Bena Kallick, and Heidi Menzel, who volunteered to read my manuscript and give me the benefits of their seasoned expertise. To my editor, J. A. Senn, I offer my gratitude for using her skill and good humor to help me complete this project. Finally, I would like to thank my husband Martin, who responded to computer and photocopier breakdowns with alacrity, and more important, who understood the demands that writing entails.

Table of Contents

 Preface

When I think of the ways I have evaluated reading in over 20 years as an elementary teacher, I am amazed at the changes that have taken place in just the last several years. To be honest, when I first began using a literature-based approach, I knew very few ways to find out what my students really knew about reading and the ways stories function. Consequently, I turned to tools that would produce concrete numbers: a multiple choice reading test in September and a commercial reading program that provided brief texts and quizzes on color-coded cards at a range of reading levels for the rest of the school year. Although the students' scores and color levels gave me information I believed I needed for report card evaluations, they were not at all useful for showing me how to help the children become better readers. What's more, the processes of comprehension--the ways readers make meaning out of a text—were a complete mystery to me.

As more teachers in my district began making the transition from basals to literature, they too became aware that these traditional methods for evaluating reading did not match what we were teaching. Our reading classrooms were exciting literacy-rich places where a lot of learning was going on, but the problem, of course, was that we had very little real evidence to prove it. We needed practical tools and procedures that would enable us to gather information about the progress our students made as they went about selecting books, writing in response logs, keeping book records, discussing books, and working on a wide variety of literature activities and projects.

With the help of a curriculum summer grant, the other teachers and I immersed ourselves in current literature about reading assessment. For example, using Goodman, Watson's, and Burke's *Reading Miscue Inventory*, we taught ourselves how to do a miscue analysis of a running record; and from Marie Clay's *Concepts About Print*, we learned which strategies to look for while observing young children.

The following year this same group of teachers and I continued to work together in a year-long staff development program that was offered by our school district's teacher center. Through our course work, we learned more about authentic assessment from experts such as Grant Wiggins, Ted Chittenden, and Bena Kallick, and we generated a variety of assessment tools to try out in our classrooms. Gathering information and conducting observations, of course, were not easy at first, but with time and practice we got better doing both. By June of that year, each of us had selected and adapted several tools and procedures that were useful and manageable for us and our students.

Many of the ideas and strategies in this book were drawn from those explorations—while others are the results of teachers' experiences in different classrooms and school districts throughout the country. Because there are more assessment tools in this book than any one teacher could possibly use, you will need to be selective. Look for those strategies and materials that suit you—ones that you can adapt to fit your own reading program and the learners in your classroom.

🪭 Introduction 🪭

by Dorothy Strickland

hroughout the United States, educators are thoughtfully reconsidering many of the assumptions underlying their literacy programs. They are reviewing what is known about how children best learn and how they are best taught. One of the most significant and visible changes brought about by this reflection is the increased use of literature as a major component of the curriculum. The move toward literature-based reading, in particular, has brought much to celebrate. It has brought numerous challenges as well.

Perhaps the greatest challenge resides in the issues surrounding assessment and evaluation affecting all aspects of literature-based instruction. As schools move toward more holistic, literature-based curricula, the mismatch between instruction and assessment frequently causes tremendous anxiety among teachers and administrators. Tests of isolated skills no longer reflect the breadth and depth of what is being taught. Educators soon recognize the need for assessments that help students demonstrate what they know and what they can do within the framework of whole texts and authentic applications of reading and writing— the hallmark of quality literature-based reading programs.

In *Practical Assessments for Literature-Based Reading Classrooms*, Adele Fiderer provides educators with precisely what is needed to insure that assessment works hand-in-hand with instruction in the literature-based curriculum. Remarkably, in one volume, Fiderer manages to bring together the most valued ways known to date about how to gather information about children's literacy development. Most important, this book helps teachers make sense of the information they gather and make use of it to inform instruction. The material is organized in a manner that even a novice teacher can access easily. Experienced teachers will also find the organization of the book helpful as they seek to pick and choose among the comprehensive material offered. Grounded in sound theoretical principles, *Practical Assessments for Literature-Based Reading Classrooms* addresses a key area of need in today's classrooms in a uniquely straightforward and uncomplicated manner.

Dorothy S. Strickland
State of New Jersey Professor of Reading
Rutgers University

Creating
Readers' Profiles

*T*ake a moment to think of the different ways you observe your students as they read, write, and talk about their books. Perhaps you jot down your impressions as you listen to a child read, or you save work samples collected during the natural flow of classroom activities. If so, you probably have already discovered how useful just these few assessment strategies can be at report card time when you need to make judgments about each child's learning. Of course, the better your process of gathering information that documents a child's learning, the clearer the picture you will get about each child as a reader and the easier and more accurate your evaluations will be. In addition, as you learn where your students have been, where they are now, and what they need to learn next, the more effective your teaching will be. This chapter will help you discover where your students have been—their past experiences as readers.

GATHERING INFORMATION

The saying "A parent is the child's first teacher" is right on the mark according to reading researchers Dorothy Strickland and Denny Taylor. Children who learn to read early are usually the ones who have been read to at home. Storybook experiences, these researchers tell us, give children a resource for building background knowledge, language, a sense of story, and a love for reading. Because it's so important to begin "where the children are" early in the school year, many teachers collect information about their students' attitudes toward reading, their preferences, and reading processes—as well as their home and school experiences with reading and literature through interviews and surveys and from the parents themselves.

Actually, anyone just getting started with assessment will find that creating readers' profiles is an easy and enjoyable way to begin the school year. Interviews and surveys speed up the process of getting to know children and help provide ways to best meet students' instructional needs. However, you should not try to do too much at the beginning. In fact, just acquiring one or two new tools will give you more background information on each student than you have ever had before. (At the end of this chapter, you will find a list of supplies for organizing the various forms, work products, and records that you and your students will generate throughout the year.)

To get children to be reflective and honest about their experiences and attitudes, you will need to provide examples of these behaviors. One way to do this is to share a story about yourself when you were a student. For example, I tell children how embarrassed I was when I lost my place just as it was my turn to read aloud, and my teacher warned that if it ever happened again, I'd be moved out of the Bluebird group. I felt terrible because the Bluebirds were the best readers. Of course, you also need to include successes as well as problems.

Another way to help your students begin to think about themselves as readers is to read them some picture books or excerpts from novels and memoirs—such as those below—and then discuss any personal experiences that the stories bring to mind. Don't hesitate to use picture books even if you teach middle and upper elementary grades because they will bring back memories from readers of all ages.

After discussing personal reading experiences that the books bring to mind, you may want to ask your students to write about them. Figure 1, on page 13, shows a second grader's responses to questions about how she learned to read.

Interviews

One of the best ways to gather information for readers' profiles is to interview your students. The first step when planning a series of interviews is figuring out the questions you want to ask. You will find examples of interview and survey forms on pages 19-27 [Figures 3-

PICTURE BOOKS
The Little Old Man Who Couldn't Read by I.S. Black (Whitman, 1968).
The Wednesday Surprise by Eve Bunting (Houghton Mifflin/Clarion, 1990).
First Grade Takes a Test by Miriam Cohen (Greenwillow, 1980).
When Will I Read by Miriam Cohen (Greenwillow, 1977).
I Can Read with My Eyes Shut by Dr. Suess (Random Books, 1978).
Daniel by J. Hessell (Rigby Literacy 2000, 1991).
The Day of Ahmed's Secret by T.P. Hilde and J. H. Gilleland (Lothrop, Lee, Shepard, 1990).

Arthur's Prize Reader by Lillian Hoban (Harper & Row, 1978)
Amber on the Mountain by Tony Johnston (Dial, 1994)
I Hate to Read by Rita Marshall (Creative Editions, 1992).

CHAPTERS IN NOVELS AND MEMOIRS
Matilda by Roald Dahl (Puffin, 1988) Chapter 1.
Little by Little: A Writer's Education by Jean Little (Puffin, 1989) Chapter 12.
One Writer's Beginnings by Eudora Welty (Harvard University Press, 1984) pp. 5-12.

10]. If these forms don't seem to be appropriate for your students, you may want to design your own form by selecting questions from the list on page 14 that seem to fit your purposes and your students' developmental levels. (Use the blank form on page 27 [Figure 10] for writing the questions you select.)

If you choose one question from each of the categories on the list on page 14, you're more likely to get a broad view of your students as readers. Focusing on just one or two categories, on the other hand, will give you a more in-depth perspective of one aspect of each reader's attitudes and experiences.

To make your students feel more comfortable about being interviewed, you could tell them that you would like to learn more about them and their experiences with reading and books. Let them know that you will make notes during the interview to help you remember the interesting things they tell

Name: Lindsey.

I Can Read
When did you start to read? How did it happen?
I learnt to read mostly in the bigining from my Dad. See he was not really in to reeding wen he was ung, but now he thing's reading is the most imPortint after his family, and his job. →
So you see ever nite he would read to me or I would reed to him and that helpt.

Courtesy of Valerie Rein, Grade 2 Teacher, Heathcote School

you. Allow seven to ten minutes for each interview while the rest of your students are reading independently or engaged in a task they can manage on their own. If you teach young children, you may want to have another adult in the classroom—perhaps a parent volunteer—to be available in case any child needs assistance.

It's a good idea to ask your questions in a conversational tone, leaving plenty of wait time for the child to think about a response. One way to get more detailed information is to follow up a child's response with a comment or question such as, "How come?" or "What makes you think that?" To encourage a student to elaborate on a response, you also could "play back" the student's words: "So you read stories to your little sister. That sounds really interesting. I'd love to hear more about that." If your students have so much to tell you that you will have trouble fitting your notes onto the question form, consider recording your notes on a separate sheet of lined paper after the number that precedes each interview question. A word of advice: Because you may become absorbed in your students' stories, keep a wristwatch on the table during interviews to help you stick to your schedule.

Although conducting 20 to 30 interviews, doing a few each day, has taken me as long as two or three weeks, I find the time spent is definitely worthwhile. My students always seem to enjoy our conversations, and I get to know them and their reading backgrounds much sooner and better than in past years when it was a struggle just to remember everyone's name that early in the fall. More than just fact-hunting, conducting interviews helps you to get to know your students better and allows you the opportunity to form understandings that will become the basis for productive teacher-student relationships.

PERSONAL ATTITUDES
◆ How do you feel about reading?
◆ What is special about reading to you?
◆ What do you like least about reading?
◆ What helps you understand a story better—when someone reads it to you or when you read it on your own?
◆ How would you finish this sentence? Reading is . . . .
◆ What kind of reader do you think you are?

HOME EXPERIENCES
◆ About how many books would you say you own? Where did you get them?
◆ What do you read at home—things such as books, magazines, ads, and/or directions?
◆ What book are you reading at home now? Why did you choose it?
◆ What do you remember about being read to? Does anyone still read to you? What book has someone read to you recently?
◆ When did you start to read? How did it happen?
◆ Where do you like to be when you are reading at home?
◆ Who do you see reading in your house?

SCHOOL EXPERIENCES
◆ What helped you learn to read in school?
◆ What do you remember about reading in earlier grades?
◆ What was the best book you ever read last year, or what was the best book ever read to you last year? What made it so good?
◆ Did you ever write about an author? Can you tell me about that time?
◆ What is hard about reading for you?
◆ Did you like reading a book in groups or did you prefer reading alone?

◆ Did you ever keep a response journal or literature log? What did you write in it? Did you ever think or write about the author's message? Give an example.
◆ Were you ever asked to read aloud? How do you feel about reading aloud?

PREFERENCES
◆ Who is your favorite author?
◆ Have you ever read a book more than once? Which one(s)?
◆ What kinds of books do you like to read most? Which is the best one of all those you have read?
◆ Do you have a favorite series?

THE READING PROCESS
◆ What is hard about reading for you?
◆ How do you choose a book?
◆ What do you do if you don't know a word? What do you do if you get stuck many times on one page?
◆ What makes you decide to stop reading a book?
◆ Did you ever read the same book more than once? Is there a book you have read that you would like to read again?
◆ What is the most comfortable way for you to read?

PERSONAL GOALS
◆ What kinds of books do you think you would like to read this year? What are the titles of books you would like to read? What makes you want to read them?
◆ What do you think you need to do to become a better reader this year?
◆ What are some things you would most like to see happen with your reading this year?

Interviews also supply important information that you can share with parents. For example, my interview notes on page 15 [Figure 2b], gave me specific information to share with Eric's mother at our first conference.

After we discussed his favorite books and authors and his feelings about reading, I told his mother how much Eric enjoyed eavesdropping as she read the Miss Nelson books to his little brother. Surprised and delighted, his mother said she would look for read-alouds that would be appropriate for both boys. Many parents, like Eric's mother, need to know what an important role they play in shaping their children's attitudes toward books and reading.

Surveys

Surveys take much less time to conduct than interviews because all of your students can write their responses at the same time. You can even use surveys with young children if you read the questions and statements aloud to them. However, because most youngsters tend to share more when they talk than when they write, you probably will find that you won't get as much information from a survey as you would from an interview. Nevertheless, because time is such an important factor to consider, many teachers prefer surveys, and they use several strategies—including the following—to draw out more thoughtful responses.

◆ **Break apart big questions.** When writing questions for your survey, try to break up the big interview questions that appear on page 14 into smaller parts. For example, instead of just writing, "What kinds of books do you like to read?" give your students several choices—such as realistic, mystery, fantasy, and picture books—so that they can place checks next to their preferences or write the titles of books they have read in that genre.

◆ **Follow-up conferences.** Follow up interesting or provocative responses to a survey question in a one-to-one conference with a student. If a response indicated a negative feeling toward reading, for example, you might want to discuss this with the student.

◆ **Use fewer questions.** If you want to draw out more thoughtful written responses, spread your survey over two or three days

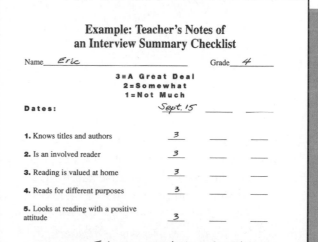

Figure 2a: Example

Figure 2b: Example

and use only one or two interview questions each day from the list on page 14. Give your students a blank sheet of paper to write on and discuss the questions with them in advance so that they will have time to consider what they want to write about. If you teach young children, you also may want to have them tell a partner about their ideas before writing. Figure 11 shows some examples of the ways second graders responded in writing to the question: What's hard about reading for you?

The children's responses to this survey question clearly indicate that these developing readers are aware of some problems—whether it is selecting appropriate books, reading aloud, losing their place in the text, or figuring out unknown words. Survey responses such as these helped their teacher know what she needed to teach next.

If you teach a middle or upper elementary grade, you can simply ask your students to write a letter to you about themselves as readers. Suggest they tell you something about their feelings about reading, their interests and preferences, and the ways their reading has changed over the years. (You may even want to read aloud the samples of the students' letters on pages 17-18 [Figures 12 and 13] to get them started.)

Figure 11: Example

Courtesy of Lila Berger, Grade 2 Teacher, Fox Meadow School

Reflections

When you encourage your students to think deeply about themselves as readers, they gain some important benefits. Whether you have asked them to tell you what they want to read this year, how they feel about reading in groups, or any other likes and dislikes, you are letting them know that they will have some control over their own learning in your classroom. Perhaps even more important, you are sending the message that it's important for readers to reflect on what they do because later on, as your reading program develops, you will be asking them to become evaluators of their own work. Although it's not always easy to determine what they do well and what needs they should work on, students who have been asked to be thoughtful about themselves as readers are on their way to becoming better appraisers of their own work.

If you have ever asked family members to share with you information about their child as a learner, you probably already know just how helpful parents' reflections can also be. In fact, a parent may be the best witness you have to a child's emerging literary development—as well as a child's interests, attitudes, and habits. One way to use parents as informants is to send home a parent survey form such as the one on page 141 [Figure 66]. Another way is to invite parents to tell you little stories about their children. For example, in notes confirming the date and time of her first conference with parents, second grade teacher Lila Berger asks them to come prepared to tell her one story about their child's early reading and literacy experiences. Receiving the note in advance of the conference gives each parent plenty of time to reflect and even discuss recollections with other family members. Following are two of the parents' stories reconstructed from Lila's handwritten notes.

◆ When Julie was 2 1/2 years old, the family went to a beach resort. One day after Julie had left her beloved stuffed bear behind at the pool, she cried and cried. The next day when another guest returned the bear to her, Julie exclaimed, "That just like Corduroy!" Her parents had just recently read her the book *Corduroy*, which is about a bear left at a department store.

◆ Jeffrey had books for all occasions—such as books to be read at bedtime, books for Nana to read, books that were Daddy's specialty, and books that only his mother read to him. When Jeffrey was three years old, his mother heard, through a closed door, Jeffrey and his father laughing so hard that at first she thought they were crying. Victor (the dad) was reading aloud *Mole and Troll*. For several nights after that, just before Jeffrey's bedtime, Victor and Jeffrey would retreat to the parents' bedroom where, lying on the bed and reading *Mole and Troll*, they would laugh until they almost cried.

The previous stories reveal information about the literary experiences, knowledge, and strategies that these children already possessed when they began the school year, and they are the very kind of experiences that you will want to build on in the classroom.

Listening to the stories parents tell about their child's early experiences with books will help you learn which children come from homes where storybook reading is valued. If you hear stories such as the ones told by Julie's and Jeffrey's mothers, you can expect that those children will continue to be involved with the books they read and hear in your classroom. You also could assume that they are ready to respond to books in thoughtful ways; for example, you might invite them to relate a story to events in their own lives, match the feelings they experienced to parts of a book, or create a favorite book graph.

On the other hand, parents' stories about their children may also reveal problems. For those students who have a literature-poor background, you may want to create a home/school connection—similar to the one described in Chapter 8—by sending books home in plastic bags for parents and children to read together. This, I believe, is the real value of assessment: in the process of learning more about your students as individuals, you discover how best to teach them.

Figure 12: Example

> Sept. 18, 1995
>
> Dear Dr. Fiderer,
> In second grade I read *Sweet Valley Twins*. I loved them. I sort of like them now. Last year and the year and the year before I read *Betsy Books*. Right about this year I, want to read some difrent author. So right now i'm, reading a book by E.B. White. Can you help me choose a book after this one?
>
> -Faith, grade 4

SUPPLIES FOR MANAGING THE ASSESSMENT PROCESS

Imagine that you have started the assessment process by administering surveys or making interview notes. Because this is just the beginning, you may already be wondering how and where you will store your forms and everything else you will collect throughout the school year. Below are suggestions for supplies that are organized according to their purpose. Although your tendency will be to prepare some of these supplies in advance, remember that any systems you start with will probably change as you find your own best ways to track your students' progress.

> What Kind of a   Sept. 10
> Reader am I
>
> I love to read. But I don't ~~like~~ to read every minute of my life. Whenever I'm reading one book I can't start on another or I'll get mixed up. Whenever I see a cover that dosen't seem like my type of book I admit I don't read it. Whenever I see a cover I do like I read the back of the book or the inside panel. But ~~are there~~ I read a book over the summer called "Number the Stars" and I loved it.
> I only read Fiction and Mysteries I don't ~~to~~ read anything ~~having jest~~ Non Fiction!

Courtesy of Judy Grosz, Grade 6 Teacher

SUGGESTIONS FOR BASIC SUPPLIES

To photocopy and differentiate one form from another, use 8 1/2" X 11" copier paper in white and a variety of pastels.

To record anecdotal notes, use
◆ 2" X 3" sticky notes,
◆ adhesive mailing or computer disk labels—several sheets,
◆ a clipboard for carrying around the sheets of adhesive labels during class activities,
◆ 3-hole punched notebook paper, and
◆ index cards.

To organize records, forms, and notes, use
◆ a 3-ring binder with alphabetized tabbed dividers,
◆ a three-hole punch for work samples and forms that will be stored in a binder,
◆ manila folders for organizing the sticky notes or adhesive labels,
◆ multiple copies of class lists (up to 14 names on a page), and
◆ a recipe box with tabbed dividers for storing index cards.

To audiotape read-alouds, use
◆ blank audio tapes—one per student,
◆ 2 tape recorders, and
◆ 6" X 9" manila envelopes for storing audiotapes.

To collect work samples, use
◆ manila or construction paper folders—at least one for each student,
◆ 9" X 12" manila envelopes,
◆ expandable accordion folders, and
◆ index cards for writing evaluations of the work samples.

To store collected materials, use
◆ shelves, a filing cabinet, plastic file crate, deep wooden drawer, or sturdy cardboard box.

Individual Literacy Interview
(Upper Elementary)

Student's name _____ Date _____ Grade_____

1. What are your favorite books?_____

_____

_____

_____

2. Do you have a favorite author?_____Who?_____

What makes his/her books so good? _____

Anyone else?_____Why?_____

_____

3. When you're home, do you read books?_____ How often would you say you read?_____

Any special place or places?_____ Where do you get your books?_____

Any other ways?_____

4. Does anyone read to you now?_____ What can you tell me about it?_____

_____

What do you remember about being read to when you were little?_____

_____

Do you read to anyone?_____

5. What kinds of materials, other than books, do you like to read? Any newspapers, magazines, ads, game manuals or things like that?_____

_____

Why do you like to read them?_____

6. How would you finish this sentence: Reading is_____

Why do you think so?_____

Interview Summary Checklist

Name_____   Grade_____

3=A Great Deal
2=Somewhat
1=Not Much

Dates: _____   _____   _____

1. Knows titles and authors   ____   ____   ____

2. Is an involved reader   ____   ____   ____

3. Reading is valued at home   ____   ____   ____

4. Reads for different purposes   ____   ____   ____

5. Looks at reading with a positive
attitude   ____   ____   ____

Comments: _____

_____

_____

_____

_____

_____

_____

_____

_____

_____

_____

_____

_____

Figure 4

My name is_____ The date is_____

Primary Reading Survey

How Do You Feel When:

1. your teacher reads a story to you?

2. your class has reading time?

3. you can read with a friend?

4. you read out loud to your teacher?

5. you read out loud to someone at home?

6. someone reads to you at home?

7. someone gives you a book for a present?

8. you read a book to yourself at home?

How Do You Think:

9. your teacher feels when you read out loud?

10. your family feels when you read out loud?

How Do You Feel About How Well You Can Read?

Make this face look the way you feel.

Figure 5

Primary Reading Survey

Name_____

I CAN READ

When did you start to read? How did it happen?

_____
_____
_____
_____
_____
_____
_____

Do you like to read? _____ **What's special about it?**

_____
_____
_____

What's hard about reading for you?

_____
_____
_____
_____

Where do you get the books that you read?

_____
_____
_____
_____

Figure 6
Background Survey On Reading (Primary)

Name_____   Date_____

1. Place an **X** on the face that shows how you feel about reading.

2. What kinds of things do you like to read?

❏ animal stories   ❏ make-believe stories   ❏ picture books
❏ stories like my own life ❏ alphabet books   ❏ chapter books
❏ about real facts   ❏ poems   ❏ What else?

3. What is your favorite book for reading by yourself?

_____

4. What is your favorite book for someone to read to you?

_____

5. How many books do you think you own?_____

6. Where do you get your books?_____

_____

7. What kind of reader are you? Very Good _____   O.K._____   Not So Good_____

8. What makes reading hard for you?_____

_____

_____

Figure 7

• •

Reading Experience and Interest Survey

My name is _____ The date is_____

Directions: Mark your choices with an **X**. Fill in long blank lines with your own ideas.

1. What kinds of books and stories do you like to read?

❑ mysteries   ❑ fiction stories that are about kids like me

❑ adventures   ❑ true facts about animals, places, and things

❑ sports   ❑ true stories about people (biographies)

❑ scary stories   ❑ fantasy

❑ poetry   ❑ books that tell how to do something

_____(Write your ideas here.)

2. A good book or story that I've read recently is_____

The author is_____ I'd tell a friend to read it because

_____

_____

_____

3. I've read_____books in the last month. I prefer to read

❑ in school during reading time   ❑ with a friend   ❑ in a group

❑ with someone in my family   ❑ at home   ❑ by myself

4. I think reading is

❑ for fun   ❑ to learn new things   ❑ for getting good grades

_____(Write your ideas here.)

5.   ❑ I read better than most kids in my class.   ❑ I read as well as most.

          ❑ I need help at times with my reading.   ❑ I find reading very hard.

Figure 8

Reading Attitude Survey

Name_____   Date_____

Directions: Make one check for each of your choices.

❏ I like reading a lot.   ❏ Reading is O.K.   ❏ I'd rather do other things.

What kinds of books do you like to read?

❏ realistic fiction   ❏ picture books   ❏ poetry   ❏ true facts

❏ fantasy   ❏ folktales and fables   ❏ myths   ❏ mysteries

❏ historical fiction   ❏ biographies (about real people)   ❏ plays

❏ science fiction   ❏ _____(write any other kind you like here)

How do you choose something to read?

❏ I listen to a friend   ❏ I look to see if it's easy enough

❏ I look at the front cover   ❏ I look to see if it's hard enough

❏ if it's part of a series I like ❏ I read the back cover or jacket flap

❏ I read the first few pages   ❏ follow my teacher's suggestion

❏ if I liked other books by that author

When do you prefer to read?

❏ in my spare time   ❏ at home   ❏ as part of my class work

How do you like to read?

❏ with friends   ❏ with kids who read about the same as I do

❏ by myself   ❏ with my teacher in the group

Figure 9

Now That You're in_____Grade, What Do You Think About Reading?

Name_____ Date_____

1. How do you feel about reading? (Check one)

❑ Love it   ❑ O.K.   ❑ Not so good

❑ I feel that way because_____

2. What kinds of books do you like most?

❑ realistic fiction   ❑ fantasies   ❑ mysteries   ❑ plays   ❑ sports

❑ biographies   ❑ adventure   ❑ science   ❑ poetry

❑ facts about people, places, and things   ❑ how-to books   ❑ science fiction

❑ _____(write your own category here)

3. Can you think of a book that you read last year and liked a lot? What was the title?

❑ Who wrote it? _____   ❑ What made it so good?_____

4. Is reading hard or easy for you?_____ What makes it easy or hard for you?

_____

_____

_____

What else?_____

5. Do you like to read any magazines that come to your home? _____Which one (s)?

_____What do you like about it?

_____

6. How many books would you say you own?_____Where do you get the books you read?

_____

Figure 10

Literacy Interview or Survey Form

Student_____ Date_____ Grade _____

Form designed by_____(teacher's name)

1. _____

_____

_____

_____

2. _____

_____

_____

_____

3. _____

_____

_____

_____

4. _____

_____

_____

_____

5. _____

_____

_____

_____

Assessing Reading Abilities

*I*f you are like me and most teachers I know, one of the first things that you do at the beginning of a new school year is to find out how well each student reads. Although it is not the easiest procedure to manage in a busy classroom, I believe that taking the time to listen to all students read in one-to-one conferences has probably been the single most effective way for me to assess their competencies.

Besides conferences, there are, of course, many other strategies, forms, and devices that you can use to assess reading; for example, this chapter includes discussions and examples of reading inventories, conferences, anecdotal record keeping, and audiotape records. Because each one of these approaches will give you a somewhat different lens for looking at a student's reading performance, you will need to consider the following questions before making a selection: What is the developmental level of your students? What is it you want to learn? How practical is a particular assessment strategy for you?

Finding enough "free" time to spend at least seven to ten minutes meeting with each student at the beginning of the year seems to be the single greatest problem of primary teachers dedicated to baseline reading assessments. Of course, later on in the school year when children have learned to work more independently and cooperatively, follow-up assessments become somewhat easier. Nevertheless, most teachers believe that the benefits of the various approaches suggested in this chapter outweigh any problems—benefits such as evidence for comparing growth over time; specific, visual materials to share with parents; knowledge of children's abilities for planning instructional groupings; and appropriate books to include in a classroom library.

CONFERENCES

I usually introduce baseline assessment conferences to my students in advance by telling them how much I enjoyed learning about their reading backgrounds from their interviews and surveys. Then I tell them that now I want to learn more about them as readers. I let them know that we will be meeting in individual conferences over the next few weeks so that I can listen to them read and hear what they have to say about the stories they read. I also tell them that I will be taking notes to help me remember what they read and say. Pointing to the small round table on one side of the room, I show my students where we will have our reading (and writing) conferences throughout the year. This table has plenty of room for my three-ring binder, a student's book, and any of the student's reading records such as a book list.

Selecting Books

The Five-finger Method of Book Selection. For the first conference, I ask my students to choose a book to read to me that is neither too easy nor too hard. If there are some words on each page that they don't know, I explain, I can see how they go about figuring out new words. To help them make their selections, I sometimes suggest that they hold up five fingers of one hand before beginning to read a page and put one finger down each time they come to a word they don't know. If no fingers are down, then the book is a comfortable book. If they end up with three, four, or five fingers down, then the book is probably challenging enough to reveal their reading strategies. Many teachers believe that the five-finger method is the easiest and most effective way to match books to readers early in the school year,

Teacher-guided Book Selections. If you teach young children, however, you may prefer to guide their book selections when you meet with them for their reading conferences. You can do this by gathering several books that reflect a gradient of difficulty and asking each child to choose one book that feels comfortable and a second book that is somewhat challenging. Reading a page or so from the comfortable book usually gives children confidence and, at the same time, helps you judge their fluency. It is, however, the challenging book, the one that has some unfamiliar words on each page, that will reveal the specific strategies and clues that a child can or cannot use. For example, by asking, "How did you figure out that word?", you will probably discover whether a student uses context (meaning) clues, phonetic (visual) clues, or sentence structure ("sounds right") clues. (You can find more information about these strategies in Chapter 3, "Understanding Miscue Analysis and Running Records.")

Making Anecdotal Records

I find that a friendly conversational tone helps my students feel relaxed and comfortable during their baseline assessment conferences. I let them know whether or not I have read their books and what I know about them. I may even ask why they selected a particular book and, if they have already begun to read it, suggest that they tell me a little about what has happened so far in the story. Although I record anecdotal notes during the conference, I react to the story as they read by smiling at a humorous part or showing surprise—just as I do when listening to any storyteller.

The notes I make during a conference become the first entry on each student's anecdotal record form that I continue to use throughout the year for recording observations of each reader in my classroom. These dated, briefly written notes may describe a learner's skills, attitudes, learning style, use of strategies, strengths, needs, progress, verbal responses, and anything else that I believe is significant to a student's development. If you are new at keeping anecdotal records, you may not be sure what you should look for and listen for in the limited time of a conference. If that is the case, after noting the date and the title of the book read aloud, simply jot down your impressions of any of the following behaviors and strategies. (For an example of a teacher's anecdotal notes made over a period of time and a blank form for anecdotal notes, see pages 37-39 [Figures 14a, 14b, and 14c].)

◆ whether the reading was fluent or word-by-word

◆ whether the student self-corrected

◆ the strategies the student used to figure out unfamiliar words

◆ your impressions of the student's understandings and responses to the story

◆ your observations about the student's strengths and needs

◆ your plans to meet the student's needs

Figure 15: Example

Anecdotal Record and Reminder List (in process)

Name David   Grade 1

Reminder List	Dated Notes
9/15 Relies on print and illustrations.	10/3
___ Reads predictable books.	David needs help selecting books. He frequently chooses the difficult texts.
9/23 Can name most letters and sounds.	
___ Beginning to use phonetic and context clues.	
___ Attempts to self-correct.	10/15
___ Recognizes simple and familiar words.	Sometimes David reads for 10 minutes or so — getting better! Needs to see the difference in words that look alike by thinking about what makes sense.
9/30 Remembers the important events of a familiar book.	
9/30 Recognizes characters in stories or pictures.	
___ Predicts story events using context and picture clues.	
___ Asks questions about the story.	
___ Draws and labels story characters and events with guidance.	what shoe
___ Selects own books to read.	want show
___ _____	
___ _____	
___ _____	

Some teachers use reminder lists—like the one in figure 15 above—for easy reference during their conferences. Such lists will help you know what to look and listen for.

You also could use the descriptors shown on pages 40-41 [Figures 16a and 16b] to create reminder lists [Figure 17] that are appropriate for your own students' reading stages or developmental levels. To use the descriptors most effectively, use the following steps as a guide.

◆ Select the descriptors that best show what your students can be expected to do. Then add your own ideas to them.

◆ Place one or two lists on the left hand side of the blank anecdotal record form on page 42 [Figure 17] and make enough photocopies for each student to have one.

◆ As an alternative to photocopying, you could insert your lists between two clear plastic page protector sheets for easy reference during a conference.

Because your conference time is limited, don't expect to make notes about all of the reading behaviors on your reminder list at any one time. Simply jotting down the date next to a descriptor—when you first observe that behavior—will give you a clear idea of each child's reading progress over time. (To learn more about the reading strategies of your students, you may also want to have them complete one of the surveys on pages 43-45 [Figures 18a, 18b, and 19].)

Whatever approach you use to guide your anecdotal recording, it's a good idea to give your students some feedback afterward by telling them about something positive you observed. Also mention what you want them to do next. For example, you could say, "I noticed that you paid attention to the punctuation marks when you read. It really helped me understand that part of the story." Or "I noticed that you used the first letter when you tried to figure out a new word. Next time, I'll be looking to see if you can use that letter to help you think of a word that might make sense there."

Using Anecdotal Records throughout the Year

If you are just beginning to make anecdotal records, don't worry about what your writing looks like or whether you have included enough information. The more you practice, the better you will get at it and the more you will trust your judgment. Because it is important that you meet with every one of your students periodically, it's a good idea to check off or write dates next to your students' names on a class list to keep track of each conference. If you teach upper elementary students, you will probably find that you need to meet more frequently with students who are experiencing some difficulty than with competent readers. Even if you take records of competent readers as infrequently as once every five or six weeks, you will be able to collect valuable specific information that you can share with parents at conference and report card times.

Later on in the year, you will also probably want to make anecdotal notes about individual students as you observe them working in a variety of settings and contexts—such as group literature discussions, story dramatizations, and writing and drawing story responses. (See Chapter 5, "Evaluating Learning through Daily Reading Activities," for more information.) As you listen to your students talk to each other about their books, you may even find yourself recording classroom vignettes and funny stories—such as the following one between two first graders, made by their teacher, Mary Hayter.

3/29 Kim shared Max's First Word with Bill.

B: Why did you choose such an easy book?

K: I'm not into hard words yet.

B. Moira and me have heard you read harder books like Arthur and Fox books.

K: I'm not really into them yet though.

B. Maybe you read it because it was about bunnies and it's almost Easter.

READING LADDERS

"A list of books that represent a gradient of difficulty that a child has read over time displays a visual record of each child's reading growth," says New Zealand reading expert Marie Clay in her valuable book *An Observation Survey of Early Literacy Achievement* (Heinemann, 1993). One way to create a reading ladder is to collect a group of five to ten books—covering a range of reading levels—that your students have not yet read. A word of advice: Once you select the books for assessment, do not make them available for general reading purposes. However, rather than remove wonderful books from your classroom library, you may prefer to select stories from literature-based anthologies or purchase several inexpensive paperbacks. You could even find stories in a set of basal readers stored in your school's book closet. Whatever your source, be sure to look for stories that have natural language and appealing storylines.

Once you have selected your reading ladder books, use the following guidelines along with the blank form on page 46 [Figure 20].

◆ Record the titles on a sheet of paper in order of difficulty, beginning with the easiest one at the bottom of the list.

◆ Make enough photocopies for each student to have one.

Making Reading Ladder Assessments

Now you are ready to meet with your students individually to find the most challenging book on the list that they can read comfortably to you with 95 percent or higher accuracy. To save some time, you may want to provide a few books in advance of the conference and encourage a child to try to find his or her hardest "just right" book. Suggest that your students use the five-finger strategy described on page 30 and tell them if, after making a fist, they come across another word they don't know, that book is probably too hard for them. In any case, listening to a child read the first few pages should tell you if he or she could comfortably read a more challenging book or should read an easier selection.

After a child book selects a book, give him or her time to skim through it prior to reading it aloud to you. Then after the reading is over, write the date next to that title on the list. If you repeat this assessment periodically, your lists of Ladder Books will give you a visual record of each child's reading growth in such as the one above.

After assessing each student's reading, some teachers select a benchmark book from the titles on the list—one that represents a text that most students were able to read with 95 percent accuracy. Selecting a benchmark book helps you know which children need additional help to reach the benchmark goal.

AUDIOTAPES

Another method of assessing your students' reading abilities is to tape their reading performances early in the school year as you listen to them read aloud in conferences. You will find that listening to a tape and hearing a child's reading a second time will also provide you new awarenesses that you did not pick up the first time.

All you need, in addition to the book, are a tape recorder and one tape for each child in your class. If the school's funds are limited, you could request a supply of audiotapes from

Figure 21: Example

Reading Ladder Books

Name _Shauna R._____

Dates	Grade Level	Titles
7._____	2 & 3	*Tornadoes!* by Lorraine Hopping (Scholastic, "Hello Reader")
6._____	2 & 3	*20,000 Baseball Cards Under the Sea* by J. Buller and S. Schade ("Step into Reading")
5. 5/20	1 & 2	*The Frog Prince* by Edith Tarcov (Scholastic, "Hello Reader")
4. 3/18	1 & 2	*Wake Me in Spring* by James Preller (Scholastic, 1994)
3. 3/5	1 & 2	*More Spaghetti I Say* by Rita Gelman (Scholastic, "Hello Reader")
2. 11/24	K-1	*Pizza Party!* by Grace Maccarone (Scholastic, "Hello Reader")
1. 9/30	K-1	*I Paint* by Andrea Barker (Rigby, Literacy 2000 Satellites)

the PTA or ask your students to bring in a tape as part of their school supplies. Following are some helpful tips for successful audiotaping.

◆ Introduce audiotaping as a natural part of classroom reading time. Let your students know that periodically you will tape, or have them tape, their read-alouds and discussions of books so that you can see how much they are improving as readers.

◆ Keep a tape recorder on the table where you hold your reading conferences. Be sure that an electrical outlet is nearby.

◆ To keep extraneous noise to a minimum during a recording, display a sign that says, "Shhh. Recording in Progress."

◆ At the end of the reading, turn off the tape recorder and label the tape with the child's name.

◆ Store each tape in a separate envelope and write the student's name, the date, and the title of the book on the envelope. If you follow this procedure, you will find that the tapes will be readily accessible when you need them for new tapings or parent conferences.

A baseline audiotaping of each child's reading performance takes very little extra effort on your part, yet the tape gives you a concrete reference point for assessing change when you make new audiotapes throughout the year. You also will find that these tapes are a valuable assessment tool that you can send home or play and discuss at parent-teacher conferences. (See Chapter 8, "Making Home-School Connections," for ways to involve parents and children in assessing audiotapes of reading performances.)

SKILLS INVENTORIES

If you teach young children, you are probably already using an inventory or checklist to help you observe their developing understanding of written language. As you read this section, decide which forms and inventories might give you additional information about your students. The more you learn, of course, the easier it will be to determine each child's strengths and needs.

Checklists and inventories are easy to use because they outline the specific strategies or behaviors that you need to look for, but they rarely require notetaking. Although you will need to meet with each child individually, you can complete all—or even just a part of an inventory—while the rest of your students are engaged in activities that they can manage on their own.

It's particularly important to repeat an inventory periodically so that you can keep track of new strategies and skills as your children acquire them. For this reason, it's a good idea to write the date next to behaviors that you observe. Following are brief descriptions of the checklists and inventories you will find on pages 47-54.

The Print Concepts Checklists [Figures 22 and 23]

Based on ideas described in Marie Clay's recent book *An Observational Survey of Early Literacy Achievement* (Heinemann, 1993), these self-explanatory inventories are used with emergent readers, children who cannot yet read. All you need besides the checklists is a storybook. Children are not expected to actually read any words, of course, but they will be able to "finger point" to demonstrate their understandings about directional sequences of texts—for example, which way a book is held and how reading proceeds from word to word, line to line, and page to page. When using the second checklist [Figure 23], ask your students to use the pointing finger on each hand to frame a word, letter, or punctuation mark on a page of the book.

Letter Identification Inventory [Figure 24]

You can use a letter identification inventory to assess each child's ability to name a letter, identify the sound it makes, and write the letter. Because students acquire these skills over time, you need to use the same inventory periodically to keep track of them. Ethel Huttar, a first grade teacher, developed a quick and easy technique to record each child's growing mastery of these skills. As a child demonstrates mastery of a letter's name, sound, or written form, she simply circles the letter with a different colored pen or highlighter for each skill. For example,

Blue = the child knows the letter's name,

Green = the child knows the sound the letter makes, and

Red = the child can write the letter.

Any commercial self-adhesive alphabet strip that can be permanently affixed to each child's desk provides another good way to take a letter identification inventory. The advantage of the alphabet strip over a form is its accessibility. Because it's always right there on the desk, you can take a brief, spur-of-the-moment inventory at any time. Just be sure to avoid alphabetical order by pointing randomly at several letters as you ask a child to say a letter's name or the sound it makes or to write it. Once these skills are mastered, peel off the alphabet tapes and affix them to legal-size manila folders. Afterwards you could place samples of the children's work and additional assessment forms inside these folders and use them in parent-teacher conferences. A word of advice: Let your students know in advance that the alphabet strips are important records that will show their parents just how much they are learning. Then remind them periodically not to scribble on the tapes or pick at their edges.

Richard Gentry's Developmental Spelling Inventory [Figures 25 and 26]

According to Richard Gentry, misspellings provide windows into children's minds to reveal their knowledge of letter-sound relationships. Because this inventory is made up of challenging words that most young children cannot spell, it requires them to draw on their developing phonetic knowledge as they attempt to spell the words they hear. Spellings on this inventory are not scored as being correct or incorrect. Instead, Gentry provides a developmental scale that determines the developmental stage of a child's performance at a particular time. (Look at page 51 [Figure 26] to see how a teacher analyzed one child's misspellings in November and February.)

Unlike most inventories, this one can be administered to the entire class or small groups at one time—a great advantage for busy teachers! You can use any primary paper or photocopy the blank inventory form on page 52 [Figure 27]. You will need to take precautions, however, to make sure that your students don't become anxious about taking such a hard "test." You can assure them that they are not expected to spell the words by saying something such as,

"Even fifth graders wouldn't be able to spell some of these words! Just make guesses about the letters that you think you hear in the words." (To analyze this type of inventory, refer to the directions and developmental scale on page 50 [Figure 25].)

High Frequency Bookwords [Figure 28]

In her article "Bookwords: Using a Beginning Word List of High Frequency Words from Children's Literature K-3," (*The Reading Teacher,* January, 1985), Maryann Eebs provides a list of high frequency words found in 400 storybooks for beginning readers. To get information about your students' abilities to recognize sight words, have them read part of the list on pages 53-54 periodically while you highlight the words they identify correctly. By using a different color highlighter pen each time, you will have visual evidence of each child's developing abilities to identify words that appear frequently in real books.

Because the Bookwords inventory is a relatively simple one that doesn't require any observational skills, you can ask a parent or even an aide to administer it. It's important, though, to remember that the Bookwords inventory is recommended as an assessment tool, not a teaching tool, because it shows you just how many sight words your students absorb when they read story books.

Anecdotal Record

Student **Gary**　　　　　　　　　　　　　　　　　　　　Grade_____

Date and Activity observed	Book title	Comments
10/19 conference; observe of later grp.	Stone Fox Gardiner	Said he selected this book because friends did. Difficult book for him. He's able to read it because I'm reading it aloud to class. Seldom participates in his group's discussions w/ David, Eric & Paul.
	Miscues	(on running record)
10/13 Conference	The King Who Was Too Busy	Can read this book on his own. I showed him how to figure out if a word makes sense before sounding it out.
	Miscues	ordered voted adored
2/14 observat. of lit. group	Call it Courage Sperry	Reading w/ David & Eric. This book is very difficult for him. He is supported by others in group as he reads. Comprehension of discussion is good.
	Miscues	See miscues noted on photocopy of page from book.
3/27	Indian in the Cupboard Banks	Reading with Jamal. Partner reading helps. Reading is much improved. Comprehension good. Very interested in story after a slow start.
	Miscues	p. 25 though/thought woodern sc/wooden became/become displaced TA despised/despised
		instant/instance pg 29. Algon sc/Algonquin okooled/occurred
		terrorsim/terrorism repredly sc/repeatedly whipping/wiping

Anecdotal Record

Student __Karen K.__ Grade_____

Date and Activity observed	Book title	Comments
10/11 Confer. w/ me.	Helen Keller Hickock	Likes biographies and Laura Ingalls Wilder series. Also Boxcar Children. Excellent reader. Needs to read more challenging books.
	Miscues None!	
12/20 conf. w/ John	When I Was Young in the Mountains Rylant	Asked good questions about illustrations. Takes risks; willing to express her opinion. "It expresses their personality and gives you a good clue about the story."
	Miscues	
1/28 Book log entry	The Dollhouse Mystery Betty Wright	Understands mystery clues. "Everything makes sense now—dolls move back to positions during murder." Notes that author takes a phrase from chapter for title. Notes italic
	Miscues	Excited: "I can't wait to finish!" Remembers our discussion of italics from "Sarah, Plain & Tall"
2/8 Book log entry	HALF MAGIC Eager	Predicts what will happen to Black Knight. Raises questions: "I wonder what will happen - is Mrs. Bick going to find the magic coin." Reads to confirm prediction: "I was right! B.K. got burned."
	Miscues	

Figure 14 c

Anecdotal Record

Student_____ Grade_____

Date and Activity observed	Book title	Comments
	Miscues	
	Miscues	
	Miscues	
	Miscues	

Figure 16a

A Continuum of Reading Growth in the Primary Grades

Directions: Cut out the lists that best match the developmental stages of your students. Add your own ideas to the lists. Place one or two lists on the blank anecdotal record form on page 42 and photocopy.

EMERGENT

- ☐ Relies on memory to "read" familiar and predictable books (word patterns).
- ☐ Pretends to read using picture clues.
- ☐ Understands directionality of print (left-to-right, top-to-bottom).
- ☐ Joins in reading of familiar books.
- ☐ Knows some letter sounds and names.
- ☐ Recognizes some words in context.
- ☐ Relies on story patterns and pictures to predict outcomes.
- ☐ Responds to books through drawings and role playing with guidance.
- ☐ Chooses books as a free time activity.
- ☐ _____
- ☐ _____
- ☐ _____
- ☐ _____
- ☐ _____

DEVELOPING

- ☐ Relies on print and illustrations.
- ☐ Reads predictable books.
- ☐ Can name most letters and sounds.
- ☐ Beginning to use phonetic and context clues.
- ☐ Attempts to self-correct.
- ☐ Recognizes simple and familiar words.
- ☐ Remembers the important events of a familiar book.
- ☐ Recognizes characters in stories or pictures.
- ☐ Predicts story events using context and picture clues.
- ☐ Asks questions about the story.
- ☐ Draws and labels story characters and events with guidance.
- ☐ Selects own books to read.
- ☐ _____
- ☐ _____
- ☐ _____
- ☐ _____

BEGINNING

- ☐ Relies on print more than illustrations.
- ☐ Reads early-reader books.
- ☐ Uses phonetic clues.
- ☐ Uses context clues.
- ☐ Uses sentence structure (sounds right) clues.
- ☐ Frequently self-corrects.
- ☐ Recognizes names/words by sight.
- ☐ Reads silently for brief periods, but verbalizes when reading is difficult.
- ☐ Demonstrates an awareness of authors and illustrators.
- ☐ Demonstrates story understandings through art work, retellings, and role play with guidance.
- ☐ Writes brief reactions to stories with guidance.
- ☐ Selects appropriate books independently.
- ☐ _____
- ☐ _____
- ☐ _____

EXPANDING

- ☐ Reads beginning chapter books.
- ☐ Reads a variety of materials and genres with guidance.
- ☐ Uses multiple reading strategies.
- ☐ Reads silently for 15-20 minutes.
- ☐ Pays attention to basic punctuation and dialogue when reading aloud.
- ☐ Demonstrates knowledge of plot and characters through discussions and writing.
- ☐ Recognizes different types of books.
- ☐ Considers story content for likes or dislikes.
- ☐ Recommends books to others.
- ☐ _____
- ☐ _____
- ☐ _____
- ☐ _____
- ☐ _____
- ☐ _____

Reminder Lists

Directions: Cut out the lists that best match the developmental stages of your students. Add your own ideas to the lists. Place one or two lists on the blank anecdotal record form on page 42 and photocopy.

BRIDGING

☐ Reads medium level chapter books.

☐ Reads a variety of materials and books with guidance.

☐ Reads and understands most new words.

☐ Reads silently for extended periods.

☐ Uses reference materials to locate information with guidance.

☐ Discusses literary elements (problem, resolution, the story's "lesson," motives of characters) with guidance.

☐ Demonstrates knowledge of authors' styles with guidance.

☐ Compares books.

☐ Reads and recognizes patterns in different genres with guidance.

☐ Beginning to express ideas about books more fully in writing.

☐ Beginning to participate in peer literary discussions for brief periods with guidance.

☐ _____

☐ _____

☐ _____

FLUENT

☐ Reads most young adult literature.

☐ Selects, reads and completes a wide variety of materials and books with guidance.

☐ Uses reference materials independently.

☐ Integrates fiction and non-fiction understanding.

☐ Identifies and discusses literary elements and genre motifs.

☐ Beginning to interpret themes and character development with guidance.

☐ Uses evidence to justify opinion with guidance.

☐ Recognizes and imitates styles of favorite authors.

☐ Expresses opinions, understandings, and questions independently in writing.

☐ Participates in peer group literary discussions for extended periods with guidance.

☐ _____

☐ _____

☐ _____

☐ _____

PROFICIENT

☐ Reads complex young adult literature.

☐ Reads a wide variety of genres and materials independently.

☐ Makes thematic statements that reflect the larger ideas of stories.

☐ Connects events in stories to historical and current issues.

☐ Interprets character development and change.

☐ Uses evidence to justify opinion.

☐ Raises thoughtful questions and issues about literature.

☐ Engages in peer group literary discussions with ease.

☐ _____

☐ _____

☐ _____

☐ _____

☐ _____

☐ _____

☐ _____

☐ _____

Adapted from a reading continuum developed by teachers in the Bainbridge Island School District, WA.

Figure 17

Anecdotal Record and Reminder List

Name_____   Grade_____

Reminder List	**Dated Notes**

Strategies That Help Me Understand A Story
(Primary)

My name is_____ Date_____

Directions: Take out a book that you are reading now or have just read. Think about the things you did or thought about to help you understand your story. Then make a check on the line before each of the things you did. You may check as many answers as you need to.

1. Before I start reading, I

___ ask someone what it's about   ___ read the title

___ look at the pictures   ___ guess what it will be about

___ look to see if it's too easy   ___ look to see if it's too hard

2. When I get stuck on a word, I

___ ask someone   ___ read the whole part again

___ skip it and keep going   ___ look it up

___ try to sound it out   ___ put in a word that makes sense

3. When I don't understand what's happening, I

___ go back and read the part over   ___ ask my teacher

___ use pictures to figure it out   ___ keep reading

___ ask a friend   ___ stop reading

4. After reading a book I liked, I

___ tell a friend about it   ___ read the book again

___ look for another by that author   ___ draw or write about it

_____

(write your own idea here)

Reading Strategies Primary Survey

If you had a kindergartner
sitting next to you now,
how would you help that child learn to read?

Michael   April 18, 1994

I wood tet him ta saidout
ther ward or skp the ward
and than go bak to tha
word also I wood tell him
to look at the prrs

I would tell him to sound out the word
or skip the word
and then go back to the word.
I also would tell him to look at the pictures.
—Michael, Grade One

Courtesy of Margaret O'Farrell, Edgewood School

Figure 19

Reading Strategies Intermediate Survey

Name_____ Date_____

Directions: Take out a book that you are reading now or have just read. Then think about the things you did or thought about to help you understand your story. Try to think of as many different things as you can.

1. Before I read a book, I usually do these things:

First I_____Then I_____
_____

(Check any of the following strategies that you also use.)

___ ask someone what it's about   ___ guess what it's about

___ look to see if it's too easy   ___ look to see if it's too hard

___ look at the pictures   ___ read the back cover or the jacket flap

2. When I'm reading and I don't understand what's happening, I usually try to_____
_____

Here's an example of what I did once:_____
_____
_____

3. When I get stuck on a word, I usually_____
_____, or I might._____

(Check any of the following strategies that you also use.)

___ ask someone   ___ skip it and read on   ___ read the whole part again

___ try to sound it out   ___ look it up   ___ think of a word that makes sense

4. After I finish a book I liked a lot, I usually_____

(Check anything else you do.)

___ talk to a friend about it   ___ read the book again   ___ take a rest from reading

___ draw or write about it   ___ think of how it was like my life   ___ choose a new one

___ look for another by the same author   ___ ask someone to suggest another book

Figure 20

Reading Ladder Books

Name_____   Grade_____

Dates	Grade Level	Titles

10._____   _____   _____

9._____   _____   _____

8._____   _____   _____

7._____   _____   _____

6._____   _____   _____

5._____   _____   _____

4._____   _____   _____

3._____   _____   _____

2._____   _____   _____

1._____   _____   _____

Series and Publisher: _____

Figure 22

Print Concepts Checklist

Name_____ Dates: _____ _____ _____

1. What is the right way to hold this book? _____ _____ _____

2. Can you show me the front cover of the book? _____ _____ _____

3. Can you point to the title? _____ _____ _____

4. Can you show me the part that tells the story? _____ _____ _____

5. Where does the story begin? _____ _____ _____

6. Where does the story end? _____ _____ _____

7. Point to the place on this page where someone would begin to read. _____ _____ _____

8. Can you move your finger to show me the words that someone would read next? _____ _____ _____

9. Can you move your finger to show me where to go after I finish reading this line? _____ _____ _____

10. When I get to the end of this page, where will I find the next line? _____ _____ _____

Based on Marie Clay's Concepts of Print *Adapted by Adele Fiderer*

Figure 23

Concepts of Words, Letters, and Punctuation

Name_____   Dates: _____ _____ _____

1. Can you point to a letter on this page?   _____ _____ _____

2. Can you show me a word?   _____ _____ _____

3. Can you point to the first letter in the word?   _____ _____ _____

4. Can you point to the last letter in the word?   _____ _____ _____

5. Look for a capital letter and point to it.   _____ _____ _____

6. Can you point to a small letter?   _____ _____ _____

7. Which letters on this page do you know?
Point to the letters you know and tell me their names.   _____
(Teacher: Write the letters the child names.)   _____
     _____
     _____

8. What do you call this mark? (Teacher: Point to a period.)   _____ _____ _____

9. What do you call this mark?
(Teacher: Point to a question mark.)   _____ _____ _____

10. What do you think this mark is called?
(Teacher: Point to a comma.)   _____ _____ _____

11. And what do you call these marks?
(Teacher: Point to quotation marks.)   _____ _____ _____

Based on Marie Clay's Concepts of Print *Adapted by Adele Fiderer*

Figure 24

Letter Identification Inventory

Name_____   Grade_____

Directions: Circle letters the child names (blue); knows the sound of (red); writes the letter form of (yellow)

W	I	L	q	r	z
M	E	X	w	j	y
N	S		m	c	
Y	F		n	o	
B	O		l	a	
P	A		s	g	
V	G		X	d	
D	Q		f	v	
C	K		e	p	
R	T		i	b	
H	Z		u	k	
U	J		h	t	

Figure 25

Richard Gentry's Developmental Spelling Inventory

Dictate the following ten words. After saying a word, use it in a sentence.

1. monster   **6.** human

2. united   **7.** eagle

3. dress   **8.** closed

4. bottom   **9.** bumped

5. hiked   **10.** typed

How To Analyze Children's Misspellings

1. Look at a child's spelling for each word. Find the error type in the scoring chart below that best (not necessarily exactly) matches the child's spelling.

2. Write an abbreviation of the appropriate developmental label beside each of the ten spellings.

3. To find a child's probably developmental level, look for the label that appears most frequently.

SCORING CHART

Precommunicative	Semiphonetic	Phonetic	Transitional	Correct
1. random	mtr	mostr	monstur	monster
2. random	u	unitid	younighted	united
3. random	jrs	jras	dres	dress
4. random	bt	bodm	bottum	bottom
5. random	h	hikt	hicked	hiked
6. random	um	humm	humun	human
7. random	el	egl	egul	eagle
8. random	kd	klosd	clossed	closed
9. random	b	bopt	bumpped	bumped
10. random	tp	tip	tipe	type

Reprinted with permission of the publisher, *Teaching K-8*, Norwalk, CT 06854. From the May 1985 issue of *Teaching K-8*.

Figure 26

Developmental Spelling Inventory

1. mostr — Phon.
2. vnvd — Phon.
3. dres — Trans.
4. dotim — Phon.
5. hit — Phon.
6. humih — Trans.
7. eel — Phon.
8. cloost — Phon.
9. BomBt — Phon.
10. tiNP — Phon.

1. Monster — correct!
2. yooniedid — Trans.
3. dres — Trans.
4. botem — Trans.
5. Miectr — Phon.
6. hyoomin — Trans.
7. eegel — Trans.
8. cloesd — Trans.
9. bumt — Trans.
10. tiep — Trans.

Name Michael

Date 11/21/94

Level Phonetic

Name Michael

Date 2/28/95

Level Transitional

Courtesy of Ellen Anders, First Grade Teacher, Heathcote School.

Figure 27

Developmental Spelling Inventory

Stage   Stage

1. _____ _____   1. _____ _____

2. _____ _____   2. _____ _____

3. _____ _____   3. _____ _____

4. _____ _____   4. _____ _____

5. _____ _____   5. _____ _____

6. _____ _____   6. _____ _____

7. _____ _____   7. _____ _____

8. _____ _____   8. _____ _____

9. _____ _____   9. _____ _____

10. _____ _____   10. _____ _____

Name_____   **Name**_____

Date_____   **Date**_____

Level_____   **Level**_____

Figure 28

A High Frequency Bookwords Inventory

Name_____ Grade_____

Color Key: fall ☐ winter ☐ spring ☐

the	what	would	know
and	we	time	help
a	him	love	grand
I	no	walk	boy
to	so	came	take
said	out	were	eat
you	up	ask	body
he	are	back	school
it	will	now	house
in	look	friend	morning
was	some	cry	yes
she	good	back	after
for	this	now	never
that	don't	friend	or
is	little	cry	self
his	if	oh	try
but	just	oh	has
they	baby	Mr.	always
my	way	bed	over
of	there	an	again
on	every	very	side
me	went	where	thank
all	father	play	why
be	had	let	who
go	see	long	saw
can	dog	here	mom
with	home	now	kid
one	down	think	give
her	got	new	around

Figure 28 Continued

A High Frequency Bookwords Inventory

Name_____   Grade_____

Color Key: fall ▭   winter ▭   spring ▭

by	us	get	took
Mrs.	should	when	dad
off	room	thing	found
sister	pull	do	lady
find	great	too	soon
fun	gave	want	ran
more	does	did	dear
while	car	could	man
tell	ball	make	better
next	sat	big	through
only	stay	from	stop
am	each	put	still
began	ever	read	fast
head	until	them	lot
keep	shout	as	blue
teacher	mama	Miss	bath
sure	use	any	mean
says	turn	right	sit
ride	thought	nice	together
pet	papa	other	best
hurry	day	well	brother
hand	at	old	feel
hard	have	night	floor
push	your	may	wait
our	mother	about	tomorrow
their	come	sleep	surprise
watch	not	made	shop
because	like	first	run
door	then	say	own

Word list from "Bookwords: Using a beginning word list of high frequency words from children's literature K-3" Maryann Eeds, The Reading Teacher, January 1985. Reprinted with permission of Maryann Eeds and the International Reading Association.

Understanding Miscue Analysis and Running Records

When you are making reading assessments, one significant behavior that you should listen for, record, and analyze is the kind of errors, or miscues, a student makes when reading aloud. Although the most common miscue is the substitution of another word for the one that is in the text, other miscues include omissions, insertions, and repetitions of words. At one time all deviations from the text were regarded as errors that had to be corrected. Then reading researchers—specifically Kenneth Goodman, Yetta Goodman, Dorothy Watson, and Carolyn Burke—showed teachers how to view errors as miscues that provide a "window into the reading process," as Ken Goodman put it.

To understand what miscues reveal about the reading process, you need to know something about the following three cueing systems that good readers use to aid comprehension.

◆ **Semantic, or meaning, cues.** Good readers try to figure out what word makes sense based on the context of the reading material. In order to succeed, they need to have sufficient prior knowledge of the story's subject matter and ideas so that they can integrate new information with what they already know.

◆ **Phonetic, or visual, cues.** These cues refer to the one-to-one correspondence between spoken language and written symbols. Readers who know these relationships are able to match letters to the sounds they make.

◆ **Syntactic, or sentence structure, cues.** For students to use this cue system, they need a knowledge of the way language sounds in a sentence. For example, in the sentence, "Sometimes a black snake came in the yard, and my grandmother would threaten it with a hoe," a child who is not familiar with the word *threaten*—but who has a sense of the ways verbs function in sentences as well as a sense of the sentence's meaning—makes a selection from a limited range of alternative verbs that make sense and says "hit" instead.

One of the most important things to know about miscues is that they are not equal; some change the meaning of the text while others preserve it.

In their small but helpful book *Evaluation: Whole Language, Whole Child*, (Scholastic, 1988), Jane Baskwill and Paulette Whitman explain the importance of looking for meaningful substitutions in the following way.

The way you interpret what the child does will reflect what you understand meaning to be. For instance, if she reads the word *feather* for *father*, a phonics-oriented teacher might be pleased because she's come close to sounding the word out. However, if you believe reading is a meaning-seeking process, you may be concerned that she's overly dependent on phonics at the expense of meaning. You'd be happier with a miscue such as *daddy*, even though it doesn't look or sound anything like the word in the text. At least the meaning would be intact." (p. 19)

Consider the following example. Christina, a first grader who seemed to be experiencing reading difficulties, read aloud the following sentences from her book *Sheep in a Jeep*: "Jeep goes splash! Jeep goes thud! Jeep goes deep in gooey mud."

However, she actually read the sentences this way: "Jeep goes sheep! Jeep goes thump! Jeep goes dreep in giss mud."

Notice that in the first sentence that the miscue *sheep* for the word *splash* doesn't make sense, but in the second sentence the substitution of *thump* for the word *thud* does. In the third sentence, Christina again made meaningless miscues using the non-words *dreep* and *giss*, words that make no sense.

Christina's miscues followed the same pattern throughout her reading of her book. She tended to err on the side of phonics and seldom self-corrected, whereas when good readers make miscues, they err on the side of meaning and often self-correct. After observing Christina's miscue patterns, her teacher was able to see that she needed to teach the child the following strategies.

◆ Ask yourself, "Does this make sense?"

◆ Look at the picture for clues.

◆ Reread a sentence that doesn't make sense.

◆ Try to self-correct.

INFORMAL MISCUE RECORDS

Miscue recording is a quick and easy procedure that can be used at all grade levels during your regular reading conferences. Allow seven to ten minutes for individual baseline reading conferences while the other students in your classroom are reading independently. Be sure to tell your students in advance that they should select a book for this conference that is neither too easy nor too hard, but one that has some unfamiliar words on most pages. To prepare for such a reading conference, you could use a blank sheet of paper, an anecdotal record sheet, or the Miscue Record Form on page 61 [Figure 29].

Another way to do an informal miscue analysis—a fast and simple way—is to jot down the errors (miscues) a student makes. Then draw a line beneath the miscue, and below that line write the word that appears in the text. Your notation should look something like the following example.

error
word in text

Also note any self-corrections by writing *SC* above the error. Whatever recording system you use, you should always ask yourself the following questions.

◆ Which cueing systems does the student use?
◆ Which cueing systems does the student need to learn to use?
◆ When making an error, does the student read silently to get the meaning of the sentence or passage, then return and self-correct?
◆ Does the student usually self-correct?
◆ Does the student pay attention to punctuation when reading aloud?
◆ Does the student read fluently or with frequent pauses?

Record your observations about these strategies as well as any other significant reading behavior that you notice. (Figure 30 below is an example of a teacher's notes on a Miscue Record Form.)

If you teach upper elementary students, you will probably find that after your initial analysis of each of your students' reading performances, you will focus miscue analysis mainly on the children who are struggling readers. Analyzing their miscues regularly will tell you which specific strategies they need to learn. You may also want to ask the reading specialist in your school to do a formal miscue analysis for a child who is having difficulty. Then both of you could discuss the results. Since a formal miscue analysis requires a story of 450 to 500 words and a typescript of the story, it's really not a practical procedure for classroom teachers.

RUNNING RECORDS

Running records, devised by Marie Clay, are another good way to use students' miscues as a teaching guide—particularly if you teach developing or beginning readers. For a baseline assessment, you can use a blank sheet of paper or the form for a quick running record on page 62 [Figure 31]. Then use the following guidelines.

◆ **Explain.** Explain to your students that you are going to listen to each one of them read and that you will be

Figure 30: Example

Miscue Record Form With Teacher's Notes

Miscue Record Of _Kim S._   Grade _2_

Title and Pages _Pretty Good Magic by Dubowskis_ Title and Pages____

Date _May 1994_   Date____

M = Meaning. Does the substitution make sense?
S = Sentence structure. Does the sentence sound right?
V = Visual. Does the substitution look like the word?

Student	Text	Cues Used	Student	Text	Cues Used
some one	something	MS**V**			MSV
the	that	M**S**V			MSV
(skipped the word)	scarves	MSV			MSV
saw	sawed	MS**V**			MSV
tires	tries	MS**V**			MSV
prayer	Mayor	MS**V**			MSV
sin	then	MSV			MSV
Rabbit	Rabbits	**MS**V			MSV
the	his	**M**SV			MSV
until	till	**MSV**			MSV

Strategies Used: _Self-corrects. Uses all cue systems. needs to attend to meaning._   Strategies Used:

Comprehension: _Can give answers to direct questions. Also said, "I noticed you don't have to be good at everything."_   Comprehension:

Fluency: _Pauses frequently - particularly when reading names. Reading sounds choppy when she's nervous. Lacks self-confidence?_   Fluency:

Needs to Learn: _- to substitute words with similar meaning - to reread when meaning becomes clearer - to "stretch" into next level books - how to pay attention to word endings_   Needs to Learn:

making check marks and other notes to help you remember which words they know.

◆ **Select**. Select several books that reflect a range of difficulty. A one-hundred-word sample is usually enough to represent a child's reading accuracy. (Such a large sample, of course, would not apply to emergent readers whose books have only a few words on a page.) Show the books to a child in advance of a conference and say something such as, "I'd like you to look through these stories and pick one of them to read to me—one that's not too hard and not too easy. Choose one that has some words that you don't know on a page." If you haven't done so already, this would be a good time to show your students how to use the Five-finger method, described on page 30, to select a "just right" book.

◆ **Discuss**. When your students have selected a book, you may want to discuss the cover and the title with them so that they can anticipate what the story will be about.

◆ **Listen and check**. As you listen to a child read, make a check for each word read correctly. Some teachers record the page numbers as they go along just in case they want to refer to those pages at a later time.

◆ **Write.** When a student makes an error, simply write the substitution over the word in the text in place of a check mark—as shown for recording miscues on page 57. Also note each unsuccessful attempt to self-correct by writing that word over the first error the child made. Write *SC*—for *self-correct*—above any error that a child corrects independently.

◆ **Use notations symbols.** You could use additional notation symbols—such as the following—after you have had some practice taking running records. However, keep in mind that you can also devise your own shorthand system.

SYMBOL BEHAVIOR OR ERROR

TTA   **teacher assists by saying, "Try that again."**

     omission

^   **insertion**

/   **pause or hesitation**

After making a running record as a baseline sample, you will need to take a few minutes when the children are not in the classroom to figure out what the child's errors, or miscues, reveal. Then, when analyzing the errors, ask yourself the following questions.

◆ Does the error make sense?

◆ Does the error have visual or phonetic similarities to letters in the actual word?

◆ Does the error sound right grammatically in the sentence? For example, does the child substitute a verb for a verb, a noun for a noun, or an adjective for an adjective?

◆ Does the reader self-correct errors? If so, count the number of times that you noted self-corrections in a line and then write it below the *SC* column.

You will soon discover that errors are wonderfully revealing. A look at your running records will give you a clear picture of the cueing systems that each student knows how to use

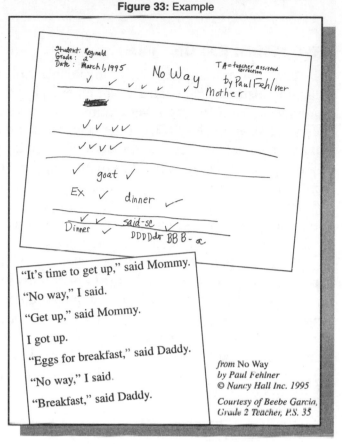
use and which systems they need to learn. Having this kind of information about your students is invaluable when planning your next teaching steps and when working with individuals and small groups. What's more, if you want to derive percentage scores for each reader, you can do it easily by counting the errors in the first 100 words: five errors = 95%; ten errors = 90%, twelve errors = 88%, and so on. Percentage scores can be useful for instructional purposes; for example, you can assess text difficulty in the following way.

◆ A score of 95 to 100% means the text is easy.

◆ A score of 90 to 94% indicates that the text is challenging enough to be used for instruction.

◆ A score of 80-89% means the text may be too hard and frustrating. You probably should encourage the child to choose an easier book.

"It's time to get up," said Mommy.

"No way," I said.

"Get up," said Mommy.

I got up.

"Eggs for breakfast," said Daddy.

"No way," I said.

"Breakfast," said Daddy.

from No Way
by Paul Fehlner
© *Nancy Hall Inc. 1995*

*Courtesy of Beebe Garcia,
Grade 2 Teacher, P.S. 35*

Your completed running record probably will look something like the one shown on page 63 [Figure 32].

Roving Running Records

Once you get some practice taking running records, you will find that you can take them anywhere, at any time, and on any text the child is reading. Paper, pencil, and a clipboard are all that you will need—as shown in the example above.

You also might want to make roving records on steno pads or sticky notepads. Simply jot down the child's name, the date, and the book title. Then make check marks for each word correctly read and write down any substitutions. You should be able to record a child's reading of 50 words or more on a 3 x 3 sticky pad and affix the sticky to the child's anecdotal record later on. On the other hand, some teachers prefer to use sticky notes only for recording substitutions above the word as it appears in the text—as shown on page 57. Whatever system you decide to use, be sure to jot down the letters *SC* each time a child self-corrects because that is such an important strategy to record.

Even without a formal analysis and score, your roving records will undoubtedly help you gain significant information about each child's reading behavior and ability to choose appropriate books. For example, roving records often highlight a child's particular difficulties—such as the frequent use of substitutions that do not make sense or confusions with word endings. This type of informal analysis will give you important information about what a child needs to learn next.

THE PROBLEM OF TIME

Although running records are invaluable tools for assessing reading performances and planning instructional strategies for emergent and developing readers in the early grades, each running record may take several minutes or more to complete. Several minutes times 20+ students equals a block of time at the beginning of the year that is difficult to find—especially when students have not yet learned to work independently or cooperatively. As a result, you should proceed slowly—perhaps by making only one running record a day or by focusing only on those children in your classroom who seem to be struggling readers.

Paired reading time—when all the children read aloud to their partners—will give you an opportunity to make several running records a day. Simply pull up a chair while two students read to each other and write your notations.

Some teachers solve the time problem by inviting their school's reading teacher, language arts specialist, or librarian into their classrooms to work with their students during reading time so that they are free to make running records with each of the students. In one school I know about in particular, the primary teachers have found an even better solution to this time problem. Their principal provides a roving substitute teacher to cover first and second grade classrooms for an entire day so that the teachers have time to make running records. These teachers feel that this released time is a truly practical gift that benefits not only them but also their students.

Figure 29

Miscue Record Form

Miscue Record Of _____ Grade _____

Title and Pages _____ Title and Pages _____

Date _____ Date _____

M = Meaning. Does the substitution make sense?
S = Sentence structure. Does the sentence sound right?
V = Visual. Does the substitution look like the word?

Student	Text	Cues Used
		M S V
		M S V
		M S V
		M S V
		M S V
		M S V
		M S V
		M S V
		M S V
		M S V

Strategies Used:

Comprehension:

Fluency:

Needs to Learn:

Student	Text	Cues Used
		M S V
		M S V
		M S V
		M S V
		M S V
		M S V
		M S V
		M S V
		M S V
		M S V

Strategies Used:

Comprehension:

Fluency:

Needs to Learn:

Figure 31

● ●

A Quick Running Record Form

Name_____ Grade_____

Date_____ Book Title_____

Directions: Make a check for each word correctly read. Write miscues (errors) above the word in the text. Write SC each time the child self-corrects.

	# SC	Errors

100 Running Words

Accuracy Rate = 100- _____ (number of errors) = _____

50 Running Words

Accuracy Rate = 100- _____ (number of errors x 2) = _____

Comments_____

_____

_____

_____

Figure 32

A Quick Running Record Form

Name _Jamie D._   Grade _2_

Date _9/21_   Book Title _My New Boy by Jean Phillips_
(Step into Reading

Directions: Make a check for each word correctly read. Write miscues (errors) above the word in the text. Write SC each time the child self-corrects.

	# SC	Errors
✓ ✓ ✓ ✓ ✓ ✓ ✓ ✓ ✓ ✓ ✓		
✓ ✓ ✓ ✓ ✓ ✓ ✓ ✓ ✓ when/many ✓ came/come	0	2
✓ ✓ ✓ me/my til/fail ✓ ✓ Kids/Kisses ✓ ✓	0	3
✓ ✓ ✓ ✓ ✓ ✓ ✓ ✓ ✓ ✓		
✓ ✓ me/my hard/head ✓ ✓ ✓ ✓ ✓ ✓ ✓	0	2
✓ ✓ ✓ ✓ ✓ ✓ ✓ ✓ take/taking carrie/care	0	2
✓ ✓ ✓ with/right ✓ ✓ ✓ ✓ ✓ ✓	0	1
✓ ✓ ✓ ✓ ✓ touch/teach ✓ ✓ thug/tug ✓ wear/war SC	1	2
✓ touch/teach ✓ ✓ ✓ ✓ ✓ ✓ ✓ ✓ ✓ ✓	0	1
✓ ✓ ✓ ✓ ✓ ✓ ✓ ✓ ✓ ✓ ✓ ✓ ✓		
/100 words		

100 Running Words
Accuracy Rate = 100- _13_ (number of errors) = _87_

50 Running Words
Accuracy Rate = 100- _____ (number of errors x 2) = _____

Comments _Uses picture clues. Self-corrected only once Next time I need to say, "Try that again." J. needs to use context to see if a word makes sense and to think about whether sentence sounds right. Also to reread silently - then return and self-correct._

CHAPTER

4

Assessing Comprehension

I n addition to finding out how well your students read, you will also want to learn how well they understand what they are reading. There are, of course, various ways you can assess comprehension. Children who make meaningful miscues, for example, are demonstrating their comprehension of what they are reading, but there are many other ways, as well, to assess comprehension—such as students making predictions, retelling stories, and writing about stories. This chapter discusses each of these demonstrations of story comprehension and suggests procedures and strategies for conducting and evaluating assessments.

HOLISTIC SCORING RUBRICS

One problem most teachers face when assessing a student's reading performance is to find ways to measure their students' comprehension. Simply writing *poor, satisfactory*, or *good*, most teachers believe, doesn't really say enough. As a result, many teachers are turning to holistic evaluation scales to help them make meaningful evaluations of their students' comprehension abilities.

To evaluate reading comprehension holistically, you need to rely on your own impressions of a child's performance and a rubric, a table with numerical ratings and explanations of those ratings. For example, following is a rubric that provides a 0-3 scale to evaluate students' written responses to the prompt: *Write about an important problem in the story. Tell why it is important.*

RUBRIC FOR SCORING WRITING ABOUT A STORY PROBLEM

Score	Response
3	The written response is complete. It indicates a very good understanding of the story and its problem. It provides accurate, relevant details, information, and supportive reasoning.
2	The response is partial and indicates a fairly good understanding of the story. Although the information selected includes mostly accurate details and ideas, some may be inaccurate or unrelated to the story's problem.
1	The response is fragmentary and indicates only minimal understanding of the story's problem. It may include random details and irrelevant information.
0	There is little or no response, or inaccurate and irrelevant details and ideas indicate a serious misunderstanding of the story.

Adapted from a rubric developed by teachers in the Bronxville Elementary School.

This rubric provides criteria that explain each number on the rating scale, and the criteria for all of the ratings mainly focus on three important features.

◆ the information selected by the student (complete/relevant, partial, fragmentary/random, irrelevant)
◆ the degree of understanding of the story problem (very good, fairly good, minimal, serious misunderstanding)
◆ the accuracy of that information (accurate, mostly accurate, minimally accurate, inaccurate)

To make specific and meaningful assessments of your students' predictions, retellings, and writings, you could use the rubrics that are included in this chapter; or you may prefer to develop your own scales and criteria. Whichever ones you use, you will undoubtedly find that with practice, holistic scoring can be a quick and reliable assessment tool. (For more information about rubrics, see Chapter 8 in Roger Farr's and Bruce Tone's comprehensive book *Portfolio and Performance Assessment* published by Harcourt Brace in 1994.)

PREDICTIONS

Anyone who reads to children—their own or their students—is familiar with the joy children take in guessing what will happen next in a story being read to them. These inferences, or predictions, are useful indicators of comprehension because they are based on a reader's (or listener's) understanding of the characters and the events in a story.

To give your students an idea of how this very important comprehension skill works, demonstrate it when you are reading aloud to them. Stop at an opportune time in your reading, make a prediction, and offer reasons for your prediction—based on information in the story. If you were reading the book *Ira Sleeps Over* by Bernard Waber, for example, you could stop at the point where Ira is listening to Reggie's ghost story and say, "I think I know what will happen next. I predict that Ira will not be able to last through the night without his teddy bear. The reason I think this is true is because Ira worried all day about what Reggie would think if he brought Tah-Tah on the sleepover date. First, he decided not to take him when his sister said Reggie would laugh, and then he kept changing his mind after that." You then could conclude by saying, "I'll finish reading the story now and find out if my prediction was right." After you have read the part of the story that reveals the accuracy of your prediction, you could say, "My prediction was right! Ira went home to get Tah-Tah."

Follow this same formula when your students reach a turning point or an important event in a story they are reading. For instance, you could begin by asking, "What do you think will happen next?" Then draw out the reasons your students have for making their predictions by asking, "What makes you think that?" You also may want to provide a more specific prompt by asking a text-related question—such as "The book says that Reggie began to tell a ghost story. What do you think Ira might do? What makes you think that?"

Assessing Predictions

When it comes time to evaluate a child's ability to predict events, you should be familiar with the story and the ratings and their explanations in the following rubric because you will need to make adjustments as you go along to fit the different developmental levels of your students. Then, after you have listened to a child's response, decide which criteria best describe the response and record the score as shown below.

RUBRIC FOR SCORING PREDICTIONS

Score	Response
3	The response is complete. The prediction is logical and indicates an excellent understanding of the character and story events.
2	The response is partial. The prediction is logical and indicates a fairly good understanding of the story. The response relates to only one part of the story.
1	The response is fragmentary. The prediction is barely connected to the story and indicates minimal understanding of the story's events and characters.
0	The response is illogical. The prediction indicates serious misunderstanding of the story.

ORAL RETELLINGS

An oral retelling is exactly what the term implies—an oral recounting of a story in a child's own words. A commonly used procedure with young children, retellings work well because youngsters naturally love to share stories they have heard or read. In addition, retellings have two other important advantages; they are not only practical but also informative. Because retellings require no special materials besides a story map form, you can use them with any story that has a clear plot. Most important, retellings show you how well a child can recall and make sense out of the important elements in a story.

In her book *Reading Comprehension: Self-Monitoring Strategies to Develop Independent Readers* (Scholastic, 1992), Susan Mandel Glazer wisely advises teachers to give children practice retelling stories before using retellings as an assessment tool. After your students have had some practice, pair them up and have one take the role of storyteller while the other one listens. Meanwhile, on the chalkboard or a chart, write the following words in a column: *Beginning, Setting, Characters, Problem, Solution.* Then after reading aloud a story that has a problem and resolution, say to the students who will be doing the retellings something such as, "I'd like you to tell the story you just heard to your partner as if you were telling it to someone who has never heard it before. Start by explaining how and where the story begins and then tell what happens next and so on until the story ends." Point to the story elements on the chalkboard as you discuss the characters, the problem they had, and the solution to their problem.

A day or so later, after reading a different story aloud, repeat the same procedure but reverse the roles of the partners. Then tell your students that you now want them to read a story and tell you about it. Remind them about the story elements and encourage them to mention these important parts of stories in their retellings. (Be sure each student has selected a story with a clear plot, problem, and resolution.)

After a student has finished reading a story aloud or silently, you could say something such as, "Now I'd like you to tell me the story you just read as if you were telling it to a friend who has never heard it before." A word of advice: A few children may need to be guided through their retellings at first. Often just a few prompts—such as those in the box—will be enough to get them going. Of course, if you offer the prompts, be sure to note the fact that the retelling was aided as a part of the assessment.

PROMPTS FOR A RETELLING

◆ How did the story begin? Where did it take place?

◆ Who is the story about?

◆ What happened in the story?

Assessing Oral Retellings

There are many ways to assess oral retellings. One is to prepare comprehension questions in advance, although this approach is difficult to do if your students will be retelling different stories. Another assessment method is to prepare a story map and refer to it as you listen to a student's retelling. For example, you may want to use the blank story map on page 72 [Figure 34] to record either what a student says or your own impressions of a student's responses. Although a student's responses may not follow the exact sequence of story elements as they appear on the form, you should still write your notes in the appropriate boxes.

When students have finished a retelling, refer to the rubric shown at the top of Figure 34—inaccurate, fragmentary, partial, complete/detailed—to evaluate their responses. Then write a score from 0 to 3 to evaluate the responses related to the individual story elements. Adding the individual scores together will then give you a total retelling score.

It's a good idea to decide in advance on a range of scores that you expect most students in your class to achieve. Some primary teachers, for example, establish a 12-15 point range as acceptable retelling scores.

WRITTEN RETELLINGS

Having your students write story retellings offers you several important advantages: it's an activity that you can do with small groups or the entire class, and it provides you with a concrete product—tangible evidence of a reading performance that will be meaningful to you and your students. In addition, you will be able to score the writing at a time that is convenient for you rather than during a reading assessment conference. Another benefit of written retellings is that you can get together with a colleague to exchange students' papers and discuss your ratings. Finally, a written retelling gives you a good idea of how well each student can write.

Primary Grades

Before you ask your primary students to write a story retelling, make sure that they first have had some practice with oral retellings. Then encourage them to write and draw their retellings using invented spellings or approximations. You also can choose between asking them to write about one aspect of the story—such as the plot's problem—or about the entire story. They will probably require two sessions for their reading, planning, and writing. The following examples of writing prompts are appropriate for second and third graders early in the school year.

◆ Write about a problem in the story. Tell why it is important.
(*Use the rubric on page 66 for scoring this prompt.*) For examples of some third graders' responses to this prompt and the planning sheet they used, see pages 73-74 [Figures 35 and 36].
◆ Think about how you would tell a friend this story. Use the story map outline [page 72, on Figure 34] to help you remember all the important parts of a story. Then write about the story on lined paper. (*Use the rubric at the top of page 72 [Figure 34] for scoring this writing.*)

Before continuing on, this is a good time to think about which new strategies and tools for assessing young children's reading abilities you may want to try out in your classroom. For an idea of the strategies one teacher selected, see her Running Record and Reading Inventory Summary Sheet in Chapter 8 on pages 154-155 [Figures 77a and 77b].

Middle and Upper Elementary Grades

For a baseline comprehension assessment early in the year, you will need to think about whether or not you want to offer your students a choice of stories or use a single story as a common text. Allowing your students to choose from a collection of several stories that represent a gradient of difficulty gives them an opportunity to be successful at their own particular levels. You should, of course, make a note of the difficulty level of the text for assessment purposes. (For ways to help your students select a "just right" story, see the discussion of the five-finger method on page 30 in Chapter 2.) Of course, providing a single story as a common text for the entire group is an easier procedure—although some students will probably find the text you select frustrating, while others will think it is too easy.

The next decision you need to make about your baseline assessment is whether or not to have your students read a short story or a novel. If you have multiple copies of a wonderful short novel, you shouldn't hesitate to use them because there is no time limit for completing this task. On the other hand, students can read a short story in less time than it takes to read a novel, and you also can duplicate a short story for each student.

Whatever you choose to give your students to read, look for a good story that has a significant theme appropriate for your grade level, a clearly identifiable problem and resolution, and a well-developed character. You are likely to find such stories in children's magazines such as *Cricket* and *Storyworks* or in any of the following anthologies. You also may want to ask your librarian for additional suggestions. A word of advice: Choose a story that will genuinely interest your students.

◆ *The Town Cats and Other Tales* by Lloyd Alexander (Dutton, 1977)

◆ *Eight Plus One* by Robert Cormier (Bantam, 1980)

◆ *Altogether, One at a Time* by E. L. Konigsburg, (Atheneum, 1971)

◆ *Every Living Thing* by Cynthia Rylant (Alladin, 1988)

Writing Prompts

Once you have selected a text or a group of texts, think about designing a prompt, or writing task, that will provide a common topic that all of your students can respond to. You could create a text-specific prompt that fits a particular story or a general prompt that could be used with a variety of texts. A story map outline—such as the one on page 72 [Figure 34]—is a good example of a general prompt that can be used with most stories.

If a task has several parts to it, write the questions on a sheet of paper and leave sufficient space between each one so that your students can make notes about their ideas before they actually write anything. Better still, provide appropriate graphic organizers—such as those on 74 and pages 101-104 [Figures 48-51]—to help your students plan their ideas in advance. Prewriting strategies such as webs, maps, and Venn diagrams almost always help youngsters think better and, therefore, write better.

ASSESSMENT FEEDBACK

To go over assessment results with your students, you need to arrange for one-to-one reading conferences, at which time you should share your insights about them and about the assessment itself. Since your goal is to help your students improve as readers, it makes sense to let them know how well they did and what they could do better the next time. (You could use any of the following questions at your assessment conferences.)

◆ How did you feel about reading this story? Explain why you felt the way you did.

◆ Which part of your answer do you think shows your best thinking? What is good about it?

◆ Which part of your response could have been better? What was not so good about it?

◆ Look at my ratings of your work. For example, I thought that you used mostly accurate ideas and details, but some of them didn't really relate to the problem of the story. What do you think about your answers?

◆ Are there any of my ratings that you don't understand? Are there any that you don't agree with?

◆ Did you understand what you were supposed to do? Is there anything you weren't sure about or anything that wasn't clear to you?

◆ What could I do to improve this assessment? For example, is there anything I could add or change in the future?

TEACHER-CREATED "TESTS"

If you like to create your own "tests," or writing tasks, periodically throughout the year to assess your students' growing comprehension abilities, you could use the prompts described in this chapter, or you may want to create your own. If you develop your own tests, try to create prompts that call for thoughtful explanations, invite personal reactions, and generally appeal to your students. It's also a good idea to show your students the scoring rubric you plan to use *before* they begin to write. Knowing your expectations in advance will help many of them produce better work.

Following are examples of prompts you could use with upper elementary students. They are general tasks that you can modify—by omitting or adding parts—to suit your students.

1. (a) Write about an important problem in the story.
(b) Tell about the different attempts the main character, or characters, made to solve the problem.
(c) Which attempt worked best? Explain why it worked.
(d) If you were the main character, what else would you have done to solve the problem? (*Use the rubric on page 66 for scoring this prompt.*)

2. Characters can be interesting people. Think about the main character in the story.
(a) Use as many describing words as you can to paint a word picture of the main character.
(b) Use evidence from the story to justify your opinions of the character.
(c) Write a letter to the main character in the story. You could offer advice about how to handle a problem, give compliments, make criticisms, or offer sympathy. Be sure to base your advice on what you learned about the character in the story.

3. Characters, like people, often change as a result of events.
(a) Write about what the main character was like at the beginning of the story.
(b) Write about what the main character was like at the end of the story.
(c) Write about the events and people that led the character to change. (*Use the scoring rubric on page 76 [Figure 37] to evaluate character analysis writing— #2 and #3.*)

Figure 34

Story Map For Retellings

Student's name_____ Date_____

Title_____ Author_____

Total Score_____ Was the retelling assisted?_____

0	1	2	3	
inaccurate	fragmentary	partial	complete/detailed	scores

Beginning/Setting (How and where does the story begin?)   _____

Characters (Who are the main characters?)   _____

Sequence of Major Events (What are the most important

things that happen in the story?)   _____

Problem (What is an important problem in the story?)   _____

Resolution (How is the problem solved? How does the story end?)   _____

Figure 35 Student Example

Response to "Write about a Problem in the Story"

Name _Daniel D_   Date _11/14_

Title _Grandfather's Walking Stik_

PROBLEMS! PROBLEMS!

An important problem in this story was
Grandfather's Kane broke

It was an important problem because
Grandfather used it as a suvanear.

Attempts to solve the problem (what was tried that did not work)
He tride to give Grandfather his toys.

The problem was solved when
thay just forgot about it.

Name _Daniel_   Date _11/16_

Title _Grandfather's Cane_

Write about an important problem in the story.
Tell why it is important and how it was solved.

Grandfather's Cane broke. The Cane was very speshal to him. The Cane broke by Danny hiting a wall wen he was playing night. He told his grandfather. His Grandfather's mouth fell open. Danny tride to give his Grandfather some of his toys. Then Danny tout his Grandfather a cowboy song. Grandfather said it is ok. Then they sang it all the way home.

Figure 36

• •

Prewriting Organizer

Name_____   Date_____

Title_____

Problems! Problems!

An important problem in this story was

_____

_____

_____

_____

It was an important problem because

_____

_____

_____

_____

Attempts to solve the problem (what was tried that did not work)

_____

_____

_____

_____

The problem was solved when

_____

_____

Figure 36 b

Writing Task

Name_____ Date_____

Write about an important problem in the story. Tell why it is important and how it was solved.

_____

_____

_____

_____

_____

_____

_____

_____

_____

_____

_____

_____

Figure 37

Rubric For Scoring
Writing About A Story Character

3   The written response is fully developed and indicates an excellent understanding of the main character. Accurate, relevant information selected from the text supports opinions and interpretations.

2   The response is partial and indicates a fairly good understanding of the character. Information selected from the text partially support opinions. Or the response may include literal, accurate details with partial evidence of interpretive reasoning. Some minor inaccuracies may appear.

1   The response is incomplete and indicates a minimal understanding of the character. Many opinions and interpretations are unsupported. Or the response may include minimal information about the character without evidence of interpretive reasoning. Some information may be inaccurate or unrelated.

0   There is little or no response. Or inaccurate and irrelevant details and ideas indicate a serious misunderstanding of the story character.

CHAPTER

Evaluating Learning Through Daily Reading Activities

The best opportunities for assessing your students' learning will occur in the natural context of your literature-based reading program. Whatever activities—such as book records, response journals, reading conferences, or book discussion groups—you consider to be particularly important for your students' literacy growth are the ones to keep uppermost in your mind as you plan your assessments.

Although you probably have ideas about what constitutes "good" student performances, you may be wondering how you can help your students develop their own understandings of the criteria for "good" student performances. One of the best ways, of course, is to invite your students to share in the evaluation process. What's more, there are many rewards that grow out of shared evaluations; for example, you will find it easier to manage your own assessment tasks, and you will have additional information to include in your own evaluations. Even more important, self-evaluation fosters the kind of reflective thinking that leads to improved learning.

Because teacher-student evaluation is such an important subject, I want to introduce you first to the following assessment guidelines that can make joint evaluation work more effective. Then I will show you how teachers apply these approaches to assessment during daily reading activities.

◆ **Focus on what a child can do.** Children need to think about what they are doing well. A positive assessment helps them know what they are learning, and it goes a long way in giving them the confidence they need to improve.

◆ **Offer specific evaluation information.** Both students and their parents need specific information to highlight strengths or indicate problems. Instead of using vague terms such as *good, poor*, or *satisfactory*, I offer specific comments and suggest possible solutions to any problems.

◆ **Be clear and explicit about expectations.** Be as clear and explicit about your values and expectations as possible; for example, you could show your students the rating sheet that you will use to evaluate their projects—even before they begin working on it. Knowing what you will look for helps students produce better work.

◆ **Build criteria together.** Involve your students in developing the criteria that will be used to evaluate their work. To accomplish this, you could share examples and models of "best" work and ask your students to think about what makes the work good. Then, using their words on charts, develop open-ended lists of criteria that can later be turned into checklists.

◆ **Involve students in ongoing self-evaluation**. Build self-evaluation into most learning activities by making it a natural, ongoing habit—rather than a special event. Start small and simple and then gradually expose your students to a variety of self-evaluation strategies and record keeping that involves them in making daily decisions about their work.

◆ **Encourage self-reflection**. To help your students understand what reflective thinking sounds like, model the process for them. For example, think aloud about how a book you have read could have been even better. Also, to make self-reflection a habit, ask your students to use logs and checklists for evaluating their learning.

◆ **Have students keep portfolios.** Ask your students to keep portfolios of samples of their very best work to date throughout the year. As they replace earlier examples of "best work" with more recent "even better" products, they will be engaging in a continuing process of reflective evaluation.

◆ **Involve parents in assessment and evaluation.** Parents become part of the evaluation process when the portfolios periodically go home. After reviewing the contents of the portfolio with their children, encourage parents to write back, offering their own insights and reactions. (For more information about portfolios, see the last two chapters of this book.)

SELF-EVALUATION

Because the self-evaluation process is such an important part of assessment and teaching—perhaps the most important part—it's an excellent place to begin connecting assessment to your reading workshops. The following suggestions, I believe, will help you implement self-evaluation in your classroom.

Demonstrating the Reflective Process

You can introduce your students to self-evaluation by showing them a portrait of a thoughtful reader—yourself. Why not share your personal reading list with them: the novels, professional books and journals, magazines, newspapers, and other materials that you have read over the last few months. Be especially careful to draw a line through any book or magazine on your list that you did *not* complete. This tactic will help your students understand that while readers do abandon books sometimes, they do so for good reasons. You also could mention the number of books you have read, but emphasize that quality and complexity matter more to you than quantity. You can continue your discussion about your reading with your students by explaining any of the following ideas.

◆ Why did you select a particular book or magazine? (had a recommendation from someone; recognized a favorite author, genre, or subject; saw a movie based on the novel)

◆ What is your opinion of the book or magazine? What are the reasons for your opinion?

◆ What are some comments and/or examples that you could give about a novel's length and the reading challenge it presented? (hard, about right, easy)

◆ How many books did you read? Why did you read that many or that few?

◆ Who are your favorite authors? What are your favorite series and/or genres?

◆ How did a novel relate to people and/or incidents in your life?

◆ Why did you abandon a particular book? (thought the characters weren't believable, lost interest in the plot, didn't like the genre or subject)

◆ How would you explain your reading habits? (where, when, and how much time you spend reading)

◆ What predictions did you make while reading? What were they based on? Were your predictions accurate?

◆ What are your reading goals? (spend more time reading, books and materials you plan to read next, genres or subjects you would like to explore)

During and after your discussion, encourage your students to ask you questions and offer their comments. Then let them know that you will expect them to record what they read and to reflect on themselves and their books in a similar way.

Building Criteria for Quality Responses

If you have been teaching for a while, you probably have already discovered that thoughtful responses to reading rarely just happen. Fortunately, there are several good ways that you can help your students understand what reflective readers do. You can, for example, show them models and demonstrations of thoughtful responses and offer them many opportunities to share their developing ideas with you and their peers. However, without such support, nurturing, and encouragement, many student responses are limited to straightforward retellings and phrases such as, "I like the part when. . . ." First, of course, you need to have a clear idea of your own goals and expectations—the knowledge, skills, and behaviors that you value enough to assess. Although your goals probably will not be exactly the same as anyone else's, you may find it helpful to know what other teachers say they have in mind when they evaluate their students' work—such as the following comments made by teachers.

◆ "Students should be able to do more than retell a story. They should be able to perceive literature on their level—much as adults do. For example, they should be able to infer the moral or lesson in a story, describe a character's motives, relate a character's actions to their own lives, and question parts they don't understand."

◆ "It's important that students should learn to figure out the theme of a novel, what big idea the story deals with. They also should be able to make comparisons—such as how a character changes from the way he or she was at the beginning or how one book compares to another."

◆ "I expect to see evidence that my students are involved with books and authors. They should always have their heads in their books during reading time, recommend books they enjoyed to classmates, reread books they love, and follow the works of a favorite author."

◆ "I want my young readers be able to draw the sequence of a story's main events, do role playing to show what the characters are like, and apply what they have read by writing an extension of the story."

At this point, you may want to take a few minutes to look at The Reading Curriculum and Assessment Planning Chart on page 88 [Figure 38a]. As you review it, think about the activities in your own reading program and the goals and behaviors you value. (To customize this chart for your students, simply write your own ideas on the blank spaces on the blank chart on page 89 [Figure 38b].) Then as soon as you have decided which reading-related activities your literature-based reading program will include, you and your students can begin collecting the information that you need to assess learning.

INDEPENDENT READING

Whether you refer to it as SSR (Silent Sustained Reading), D. E. A. R. (Drop everything and read), or independent reading, you probably set aside a period of time each day for your students to read. In some classrooms students use part of their independent reading time to update a booklist, write a response log, or discuss a book with a teacher or friend. You also may periodically want to ask your students to compete a checklist or survey to show how they feel about independent reading and the ways they use their time. For example, you could ask your students to rate how good they are at selecting books they will enjoy, how diligent they have been about writing in their response notebooks and keeping their booklists up to date, and how they are doing in other reading related activities. See, for example, the survey in Figure 39 below.

Teacher Observations during Independent Reading

Whatever activities your students engage in, independent reading time offers you a rare opportunity to observe your students at work. The following supplies, I believe, come in handy to jot down observations of students as you move about the classroom.

◆ a clipboard and several sheets of adhesive mailing labels
◆ sticky paper notepads
◆ individual file folders, a tabbed notebook, or three-ring binder for storing students' anecdotal records

After you have recorded your observations on labels or sticky notes, peel them off and press them inside a folder or onto a page in your notebook or binder. The following examples give you an idea of the kinds of information you might be able to gather as you observe your students. Although my notes appear abbreviated and disjointed, they clearly capture the meaning of a particular episode when I read them at a later time.

10/13 Danny wandering around. I suggest Charl. & Choc. Factory. D: Do I have to read the whole thing!

Figure 39: Example

How Well Did I Use My Independent Reading Time Today?

Name_____ Date_____

Title of my book_____ Author_____

Today's reading time was_____because_____
_____

I did the following things during reading time:
_____   _____
_____   _____

The thing I feel best about was_____
_____

Directions: Use the following scale to rate yourself in each area:

| 1=not so good | 2=O.K. | 3=Great! |

Time I spent reading ❏   Updating my book records ❏

Response Journal writing ❏   Other_____ ❏

My teacher can help improve reading time by_____
_____
_____

I plan to improve by_____
_____
_____

10/13 Karen: Reading Julie and the Wolves. Says Jess read it so she will, too. A bit of a reach, but?

10/13 Elizabeth and Amanda sitting together reading own copies of One of a Kind Family. Eliz.: What's a woebegone little figure? Am: Sad, maybe. Eliz. pathetic? Am: Yeah, both.

Although my notes offer only small clues about each of these fourth grade readers, you probably could guess that Danny was a reluctant reader in October; that Karen, an able reader, was willing to struggle a bit with a book if her friend recommended it; and that "buddy reading" helped Elizabeth and Amanda, both good readers, to figure out unfamiliar words. Over time, however, the picture of each student became clearer, and changes became apparent. For example, in a February note about Danny I wrote, "D has read all of Dahl's books. Suggested I read Matilda & said 'I wish he wrote more books.'"

Reading Records: Booklists and Genre Charts

Booklists, which are sometimes called reading logs, are used at all grade levels to keep track of the titles a student reads. Depending on the developmental level of your students, however, you may want to ask them to record additional information—such as their rating or opinion of each book, the author's name, the dates the book was begun and completed, and the genre. (As a help to your students, you also could photocopy one of the blank book records on pages 90-92 [Figures 40a, 40b, and 41].)

Rather than add genre records onto a booklist, some teachers prefer to ask their students to keep separate genre charts—such as the one on page 93 [Figure 42]. One way to do this is to have your students create bar graphs that display the numbers of books they read in a variety of genres. Whatever form your students' record keeping takes, you will discover that these records reveal important things about each reader.

Self-Evaluation of Reading Records

You probably will find that your students will need some guidance when they begin looking for evidence of patterns and growth in their book records. I provide the guide shown on page 94 [Figure 43] to help my students analyze their booklists and genre charts.

When your students are ready to evaluate their records, you could get them started by helping one student demonstrate the process while the others observe. For example, using an overhead projector, first show the guide for analyzing book records that your students will be using. Then project a student's booklist or genre chart on the screen as you ask the student to explain what he or she notices about the number of books read in a particular period of time—which books were challenging, whether the list shows a favorite author or series, and any changes in reading patterns or preferences. Encourage the rest of your students to make additional observations based on what they see on the booklist. Following are two fourth graders' first unedited attempts to write self-evaluations of their booklists.

◆ "In my book record it shows that I've read a lot of books but I haven't been reading to much hard books. From Sept. - Nov. I read one hard book <u>The Wish Giver</u>, but I don't think it is hard anymore. In my book record I noticed that I read more Hardy Boy books by Dixon than other mystries. The Hardy Boys used to be my faviriot series but though I still like them, I like others too like the Indian series by Banks. So now I'll try to read other books. From September to November I read 18 books and from December to February I read 19. My book record shows I love to read."

◆ "In the genre chart I notice that in September to November I read mostly realistic contemporary fiction but from Dec. to Feb, I read more different kinds of books. I need to read picture books, myths and legends, poetry, and jokes. I need to read more biography, informational books, short story collections, science fiction and plays."

READING RESPONSE NOTEBOOKS

You are familiar with current research on reading response if you already ask your students to respond to the books they read by writing or drawing their interpretations and reactions in a notebook. This approach is based on Louise Rosenblatt's theory of reading as a transaction between the reader and the text. She believes that personal reactions and prior experiences help readers make sense of a story.

One good way to encourage students to make such connections and reflect more thoughtfully on their reading is through letter writing, a person-to-person approach that was developed by Nancie Atwell in (*In the Middle*, Heinemann, 1987). Because the exploration of ideas is a riskier and more challenging task than the routine listing of factual information, you will need to establish a climate that encourages risk-taking and trust.

To introduce letter writing as a response to reading, you could give your students the following explanation of this approach—in a letter format.

Dear Student,
This year you will keep a reading notebook in which you will write letters to me about the books you read. Your notebook will be a place where you can tell me your thoughts, opinions, and questions without worrying about being correct. I hope to learn about what you are like as a reader from your letters. For example, you may want to write to me about any of the following topics, or you can choose your own ideas.

• What is something that made you laugh or feel sad?
• What is something you didn't understand?
• What do you think might happen next in the story?
• What kind of person is the main character?
• How would you rate the book? Why?
• What did the story remind you of in your own life or in other books?
• Why did you choose your book?
• What book might you read next?
• How are you changing as a reader?

Of course, there will be many other topics you might want to write to me about. The two most important things to show me through your letters is what you are thinking about books and what you notice about yourself as a reader.

Happy reading!

Sincerely,

P.S. Please bring in a soft cover looseleaf binder with paper in it to use as a notebook. From time to time, I'll ask you to take out your best letter and place it in a separate folder.

Establishing Criteria for Responses

One of the best ways I have found to help my students understand what I mean when I ask them to write responses that reflect good thinking is to read aloud examples of students' thoughtful entries—such as those shown on pages 95-96 [Figures 44a and 44b]. Then I ask, "What makes this response good?" Then using their ideas, I record what they tell me on a chart such as the following.

What a Thoughtful Reader Does
◆ describes a character's feelings and explains why they feel that way
◆ compares the movie to the book and explains how they are connected
◆ tells why the book took so long to finish
◆ tells what kinds of books to look for at a book fair
◆ tells what is going to happen next in the story and the reasons for the prediction
◆ writes about a great description, using words from the book
◆ notices that the author used words from a chapter for its title.

I leave this chart open-ended so that my students can add to it during sharing times when they recommend good books to each other or read aloud particularly good notebook entries.

Building a Vocabulary for Thoughtful Responses

During classroom mini-lessons, I gradually introduce a more explicit vocabulary for describing the processes "thoughtful readers" use. For example, I point out that the word *predicts* means "tells what might happen next in the story," and the phrase *quotes the author* is a more precise way of saying "uses words from the book." With this approach, your students will learn to use specific terms to indicate their thinking processes—terms such as *compares, describes, evaluates, makes personal connections, justifies, provides evidence*, and *criticizes*. In other mini-lessons, show students how to include literary terms in their written discussions—terms such as *setting, plot, theme, point of view*, and *author's writing style*. Before you conclude each lesson, you also might want to ask your students to sum up what they learned. Then using their words, add their ideas to a chart on literature responses that your class has been developing over time. After you supply your students with their own copies of the chart, encourage them to use it for evaluating their written entries. See, for example, the chart entitled "Building Criteria for Literature Response" on page 97 [Figure 45].

Using Sentence Stem Prompts

Sentence stems such as those on page 84 are another good way to help your students react in thoughtful ways to what they have read. Although the following stems work equally well with students in first grade through high school, the younger children will need your help to get them started.

Introducing Sentence Stems. If you teach primary children, I recommend the following steps to help your students write or draw their ideas about a book they have heard or read.

SENTENCE STEM PROMPTS

I NOTICED...

I THINK...

IF I WERE...

I DON'T UNDERSTAND...

I WONDER...

I WAS SURPRISED...

I BEGAN TO THINK OF...

IT SEEMS LIKE...

I'M NOT SURE...

SOME OF THE ILLUSTRATIONS...

I LOVE THE WAY...

THIS STORY TEACHES...

◆ Model how you would use the stems yourself during a discussion of a book you have read aloud.

◆ Tell your students that you have found that some words are particularly helpful for triggering ideas about a story. Then identify the sentence stems you used by writing them on sentence strips or on a chart.

◆ Invite a student to choose one sentence stem and use it to talk about a story. To encourage diversity, have others use the same strip and add their own ideas.

◆ Have your students work in pairs to select a sentence stem and write their responses to it. They also might enjoy illustrating their ideas.

The comments children make when responding to these stems are often surprising. In the following response, for example, a first grader inferred the moral in her book *The Man Who Cooked for Himself* by Phyllis Krasilovsky. Then she made connections between the book and her knowledge of her classmates' reading preferences. (For additional examples of primary children's responses, see page 98 [Figure 46a]. You will also find a blank form for filling in any of the stems above on page 99 [Figure 46b].)

"This book teches you that you code [should] not be lazy. I would rkmend this book to Jenny and Margot becaz Margot like's dog's and Jenny like's cats. Ther are booht [both] of tohos [those] aimnm [animals] in this book."

You will probably find that sentence stem prompts are temporary devices because as children grow accustomed to reflective thinking, they will learn to respond in more natural ways. For example, the responses on this page [Figure 46c] were written by children without any prompts.

Of course, most young children are not yet ready to identify the specific criteria you will see in their writing. They can, however, develop a self-evaluation checklist outlining

Figure 46c: Example

Small Pig
By Arnold Lobel
I Dot Udrstand
Whst Sicing In
to the Sidwok. Mens
But Naw I
Udrstand. It Was
Cement And Small
Pig That
It Was Good
Soft Mud. the
End.

I didn't understand what "sticking into the sidewalk" means. But now I understand. It was cement and Small Pig thought it was good soft mud. The end.

Katharine; Grade One

The Tiny Woman's Coat
by Joy Cowley
I like the book and I don't
know why they count to 3
when they show 4 buttons
(in the illustration).

Chris, grade one

The Tiny Woman's Coat
By Joy Cowley
I LIKE the BOOK AND I DON'T NO WHY COUNT to 3 tHEy WHEN tHEy show 4 BUth

Courtesy of Mary Hayter, Grade 1 Teacher, Edgewood School

Figure 46 d: Example

Name Matt   Date 4/24

**How Do You Rate
the Main Character in Your Book?**

Character Anastasia   Book Anastasia Krupnick
Author Lois Lowry

	very	somewhat	neither/both	somewhat	very	
good			✓			evil
kind				✓		unkind
honest			✓			dishonest
gentle				✓		violent

List additional contrasting adjectives below. Use them to rate the character. Then write the reasons for your ratings.

	very	somewhat	neither/both	somewhat	very	
cool					✓	impulsive
normal					✓	peculiar
dependable			✓			undependable
relaxed				✓		tense
easygoing					✓	jealous

My Reasons

Anastasia is very impulsive becaos She Dicided to run away the minute she heard a baby was coming. I think she's peculiar cause she says she is dumb. She's somewhat tense cause she's very eger to rite down stuff in her book (journal). And she's very jealos cause the minute she heard the new baby was coming she Dicided to run away.

84

what they can do after reading a book. See, for example, the checklist on page 100 [Figure 47] entitled "A Self-Evaluation Checklist for Literary Responses."

Using Graphic Organizers

You are probably already using some graphic organizers—such as story maps, webs, or Venn diagrams—to help your students generate and organize their ideas in a visual format. For assessment purposes, you also can use a graphic organizer as evidence of a student's analysis, or you can use one as a prewriting strategy to encourage more thoughtful written responses.

The organizer on page 84 [Figure 46d] was adapted from one in Terry Johnson and Daphne Louis's book *Literacy Through Literature* (Heinemann, 1988). This example is the work of a fourth grader who used contrasting attributes to rate a character in a book his class had read. (I supplied the attributes in the upper part of the chart and the remainder were generated in a class discussion.) For this activity, the students recalled and reviewed episodes in the story, and they thought about the main character's actions. Having to analyze the degree to which the main character demonstrated the attribute—very, somewhat, neither/both—really stretched the students' thinking.

You will find that graphic organizers are useful planning tools for any kind of literary analysis your students may be doing. For example, if you like to design your own literature comprehension "tests," you may want to use a prompt such as the ones that are shown on page 71. Then provide an appropriate organizer for the task. For instance, if you ask your students to write about the way a character changed, have them use the graphic organizer entitled "My, How You've Changed" for generating and organizing their ideas before writing. (For more examples of graphic organizers, see pages 101-104 [Figures 48-51] There is a blank organizer on page 74.)

Encouraging Self-Evaluation Processes

The best evaluators of response notebooks are your students themselves, and the best tool is sticky notes. If your students are not used to evaluating their own work, you will need to get them started as quickly as possible. Let them know that after you collect their reading notebooks once every few weeks, you will write back to them, responding to one of their entries. When you find an example of the child's best thinking, point out in your note what you notice the student is able to do. You might, for example, write something such as the following.

> *Dear Karen,*
> *I think that this was one of the most interesting letters you've written so far. You noticed where the writer found a title for the chapter. You also predicted that Amy would get clues from the dolls. The Talking dolls! Your book sounds exciting.*

Periodically, your students should reread their reading response notebooks to look for entries that represent their best thinking. Encourage them to refer to a list of criteria generated earlier—such as the one on page 97 [Figure 45], but let them know that they should add new criteria to the chart when they are describing their own particular entry.

When your students locate a "best" response, ask them to determine the criteria it reveals and write a brief description of it on a sticky note–For example:

"I quote the author's words, or"
"This connects the story to my life."

Then the student should place the sticky note at the top or side of the page as a tab. Sometimes students will select a letter that you commented on earlier and even paraphrase your words. Encourage them to continually look for new "best" entries that they can mark with sticky tabs and share with their classmates.

Preparing "Best Work" Collections

To prepare for a parent conference or a home report, students may place three examples of their best work in a manila folder along with other work developed in reading related activities as evidence of their progress. They can write their evaluations for you and their parents and attach their work samples this along with any peer evaluations. Provide the self-evaluation survey form on page 87 [Figure 52], index cards, or special cover sheets–see example 53.

You may want to have your students include their reading response writings and evaluations with additional reading and writing "best work" samples in showcase portfolios that can share with their parents at report card times. (Chapter 7, "Showcasing Portfolios," discusses portfolios in greater detail.)

Self-evaluation may start students on their journey toward becoming literary persons who read widely and thoughtfully.

Developing Teacher Evaluations

Several factors that you should consider as you develop your own evaluations:

◆ Does the reading notebook show that a student is involved with books and reading?
◆ How developed and thoughtful are the notebook entries?
◆ Does the notebook show evidence of a student's commitment and diligence through regular habits of writing complete entries?

For a quick holistic scoring approach based on these factors, use the Response Notebook Evaluation Rubric on this page.

Figure 52: Example

My best work is dated _Feb 1_ .
I think it is the best because _____
I predicted about what will come next in Sign of the Beaver and I didnt just predict but I made some connections to the picture on the book's cover to make it make sense.

My best work is dated _Feb 11_ .
It shows
what a movie called "How the Beaver stole Fire" has in common with a book called "Sign of the Beaver". It is my most thoughtful letter because I was the only one who noticed the trick connection where Ben pretended to be a friend but stole Matt's rifle just like the beaver pretended to be dead but then jumped up and stole fire from the sky people.

Figure 53: Example

Response Notebook Evaluation Rubric
(Upper Elementary)

3 Many responses are well-developed and demonstrate reflective thinking processes. Ideas usually are supported with explanations or evidence from the story. The student's strong involvement with books and reading is apparent. The number of responses indicates that the student has a strong commitment to response writing.

2 Although some responses may be developed with supportive explanations and information, most are on a literal level with little evidence of reflective thinking. Responses indicate an adequate involvement with books and reading. The number of written responses is acceptable.

1 Most of the responses are on a literal level with few explanations. There is little or no evidence that the student has tried to reflect thoughtfully on a book or interpret ideas. The number of responses may be fewer than expected.

0 Inaccurate and irrelevant details indicate a serious misunderstanding of stories. Or there are too few responses to make an evaluation.

Figure 52

A Self-Evaluation Survey
(Upper Elementary)

Name_____ Date_____

What My Responses to Literature Show About Me As A Reader

a. My best entry is dated_____. I think it's my best because_____

_____

_____

_____

_____

_____

_____

b. Here's an example of something important I wrote in that entry. (Quote yourself).

_____

_____

_____

_____

_____

c. My second best entry is dated_____. I think it's pretty good, too, because_____

_____

_____

_____

_____

_____

d. It could have been even better if I_____

_____

_____

_____

_____

Reading Curriculum and Assessment Planning Chart Example:

Teacher_____ Grade __4__

Components (Activities)	My Goals (Expectations)	Assessments (Strategies, tools)
independent reading time, booklists, ____ (write component here) reading records	Loses himself/herself in books, selects appropriate books, reads extensively, reads a variety of books and authors. Keeps accurate records.	survey on use of reading time, book records - self-evaluations
reading response notebook	writes reflective, thoughtful entries, discusses characters and story elements, reacts to beautiful language, asks questions, writes regularly	"Best entry" self-evaluation notes, teacher's "Rubric for Evaluating Notebooks"
reading conferences	uses multiple reading strategies, demonstrates good understandings of books, reads fluently, conveys feelings about a story.	Anecdotal Record Form, Audiotape
Literature study groups	Prepares for meetings, raises important ideas, askes questions, participates in discussions, offers opinions and gives reasons.	Students' self-evaluation on "Literature Study Record Form" Make my own notes while observing a meeting.
book projects	bases project on important ideas and accurate information, displays ideas with care, shows originality	Student and Teacher Project Evaluation Forms, photographs, Planning web

Reading Curriculum and Assessment Planning Chart

Teacher_____   Grade_____

Components (Activities)	**My Goals** (Expectations)	**Assessments** (Strategies, tools)
_____ (write component here)		
_____		
_____		
_____		
_____		
_____		

_____'s Booklist

Name

Titles	My Feelings About the Book			Dates
				Started - Finished
	🙂	😐	🙁	
	🙂	😐	🙁	
	🙂	😐	🙁	
	🙂	😐	🙁	
	🙂	😐	🙁	
	🙂	😐	🙁	
	🙂	😐	🙁	
	🙂	😐	🙁	
	🙂	😐	🙁	
	🙂	😐	🙁	
	🙂	😐	🙁	
	🙂	😐	🙁	
	🙂	😐	🙁	

My favorite book on this list is

_____

My Booklist

Name_____ Grade_____

Dates start/finish	Title and Author	What I think about the book ★　★★　★★★　★★★★ *poor* ————————▶*great!*

Figure 41

Book Record

Name_____   Grade_____

1=easy
2=medium
3=challenge

Title	Author	Dates Start-Finish	1,2, or 3?

My favorite book on this page is_____

My favorite author is_____

Figure 42

Reading Genre Chart

Name_____   School Year_____

Number of Completed Books

	1	2	3	4	5	6	7	8	9	10
historical fiction										
science fiction										
informational books										
picture books										
memoirs/ biographies										
fantasy										
realistic fiction										
myth/legend folktale										
plays										
short story collections										
"how-to" books										

Yellow	Red	Blue
Sept.- Nov.	Dec.- March	April - June

Figure 43

What Do Your Book Records Show About You As A Reader?

1. **Study your booklist and make notes about:**

a. the number of books you've read and why you've read so many or so few

_____

_____

b. their level of reading challenge (challenging, medium, easy)

_____

_____

c. your favorite author and why you like that author

_____

_____

d. your favorite series and why you like it

_____

_____

e. any changes you notice from September to the present time

_____

_____

f. the titles of books you plan to read next and why you want to read them

_____

_____

_____

2. **Study your genre graph and make notes about**

a. the kinds of books you chose to read from September through November

_____

_____

b. the kinds of books you read later on in the year

_____

_____

c. the changes you see in your choices

_____

_____

d. the kinds of books you plan to read next?

_____

_____

● ●

Examples of Upper Elementary Students'
Responses to Literature

12/12

One book I especially liked is Freckle Juice by Judy Blume. I like the way she brought me into the book as soon as I started reading it. She wrote how a boy looked at the person who sat in front of him in school and counted his freckles. He wished he had freckles too because he thought they were cool. I think Judy Blume is a very good writer.

Amy, Grade 4

2/11

Yesterday I abandend (sic) "Call of the Wild" because it was a very complicated book. I was on page 24 after reading 2 hours because I had to keep on reading chapters over. I couldn't at first understand why I couldn't get it, [because] my mom read it and recommended it to me.
P.S. My mom read it in college.

Danny, Grade 4

4/25

The Whipping boy (by Sid Fleischman) is similar to the story I wrote because prince brat and my character Ralph both do destructive things and are very bossy. Except for one minor detail and that is that in the end one of them changes. I'll let you read the two books to find out who [changes].

Daniel, Grade 4

6/3

I am reading a book called Super Fudge. Fudge is in kindergarten he is very mischufis. Once he called this teacher rat face. But every one still likes Fudge better than his brother peter. Why do you think the author made the mischufis brother more popular than the good brother.

Eric, Grade 4

Dear Mrs Weiss   11/04/92
                    The Book I have
been reading, "The Loner," I think is
boring. I think this because the characters
are not very strong, the story goes
very slowly and it isn't my kind
of book. I like comedy, mystery and
private criticism books.

                    from Georgie.

Dear Georgie,   November 4, 1992
          Those are wonderful reasons
for changing books. I hope you enjoy
Cracker Jackson. If not, please see
me.

                    Sincerely,
                    Mrs Weiss

Courtesy of Joelle Weiss, Grade 5 Teacher, Edgewood School

Figure 45

Building Criteria For Literature Response (Upper Elementary)

When We Write About Our Reading, We Might...

◆ describe what we wonder about or don't understand (question)

◆ guess what might happen in the story (predict)

◆ tell whether our predictions were right (confirm)

◆ tell what a character is like and offer evidence for our opinions (describe and justify)

◆ copy words or phrases that we like (quote)

◆ tell what or who the story reminds us of in our own lives (make personal connections)

◆ figure out the big idea or theme the author may be trying to get across to us (analyze)

◆ describe the story's problem and how it was solved (explain)

◆ tell what we'd have done differently if we were the author (invent)

◆ list the subjects and situations a particular author writes about in different books (analyze)

◆ explain what makes one book better or worse than another (evaluate and compare)

◆ describe the way an author writes beginnings, endings, chapter titles (analyze)

◆ show how two characters are alike and different (compare)

◆ rate the book and give the reasons for our opinion (evaluate and justify)

◆ tell why we chose a book (explain)

◆ name someone we'd recommend a book to and why (infer and justify)

◆ point out any changes we notice in our preferences for books, series, genres, or authors (analyze)

◆ give reasons for abandoning a book (justify)

◆ tell what we plan to read next (plan)

◆ the kind of help we'd like our teacher to give us (analyze and plan)

Examples of Primary Students' Responses
to Literature Using Sentence Stems

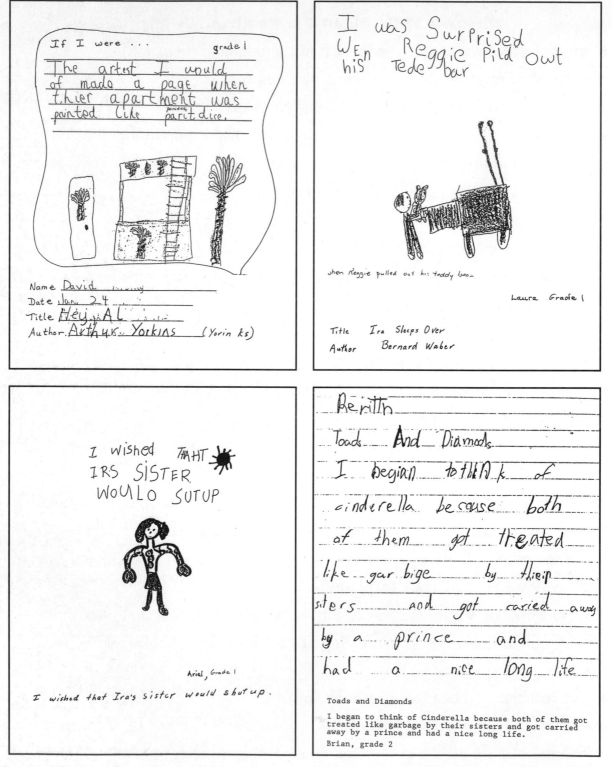

If I were ...   grade 1

The artest I would
of made a page when
thier apartment was
painted like paritdice.

Name David
Date Jun 24
Title Hey AL
Author Arthur Yorkins   (Yorin ks)

I was Surprised
WEn Reggie Pild owt
his Tede bar

when Reggie pulled out his teddy bear

Laura Grade 1

Title   Ira Sleeps Over
Author   Bernard Waber

I wished THAHT
IRS SISTER
WOULO SUTUP

Ariel, Grade 1

I wished that Ira's sister would shut up.

ReritH

Toads And Diamods

I begian to tHink of
cinderella because both
of them got treated
like gar bige by thein
siters and got caried away
by a prince and
had a nice long life

Toads and Diamonds

I began to think of Cinderella because both of them got
treated like garbage by their sisters and got carried
away by a prince and had a nice long life.
Brian, grade 2

Courtesy of Margaret O'Farrell, First grade Teacher, Edgewood School and Lila Berger, Second Grade Teacher, Fox Medow School

Response Activity Form (Primary)

What I think about the story I just heard or read:

If I were...

_____

_____

_____

_____

Name_____ Date_____

Title_____

Author_____

Figure 47

A Self-Evaluation Checklist for
Literature Responses (Primary)

Name_____ Date_____

When I finish a book, I can:

❑ tell someone the most important parts of the story

❑ list or draw the most important parts of the story

❑ act like a character in the story

❑ add a new part to the end of the story

❑ write/draw something that surprises me

❑ write/draw something that I noticed

❑ write/draw what I would do if I were the author or illustrator

❑ write what I didn't understand

❑ make a mark to show how easy, just right, or hard the book was for me

❑ show whether I thought the book was great, OK, or poor

❑ name someone who would like the book

Figure 48

Character Web

Book title and author _____

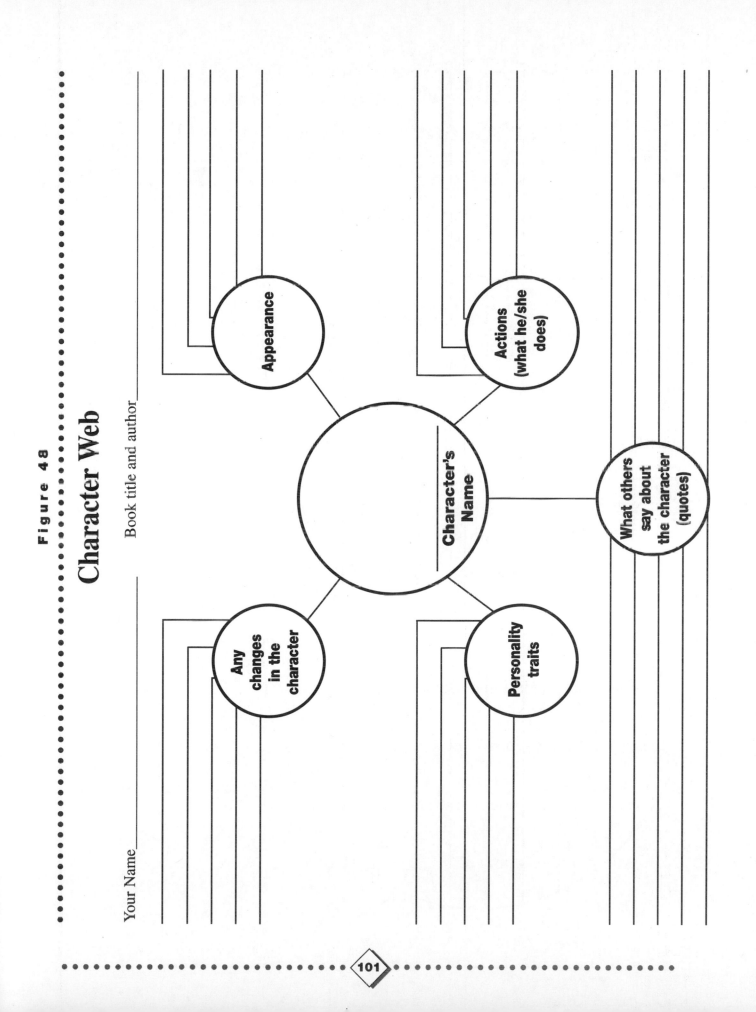

Your Name _____

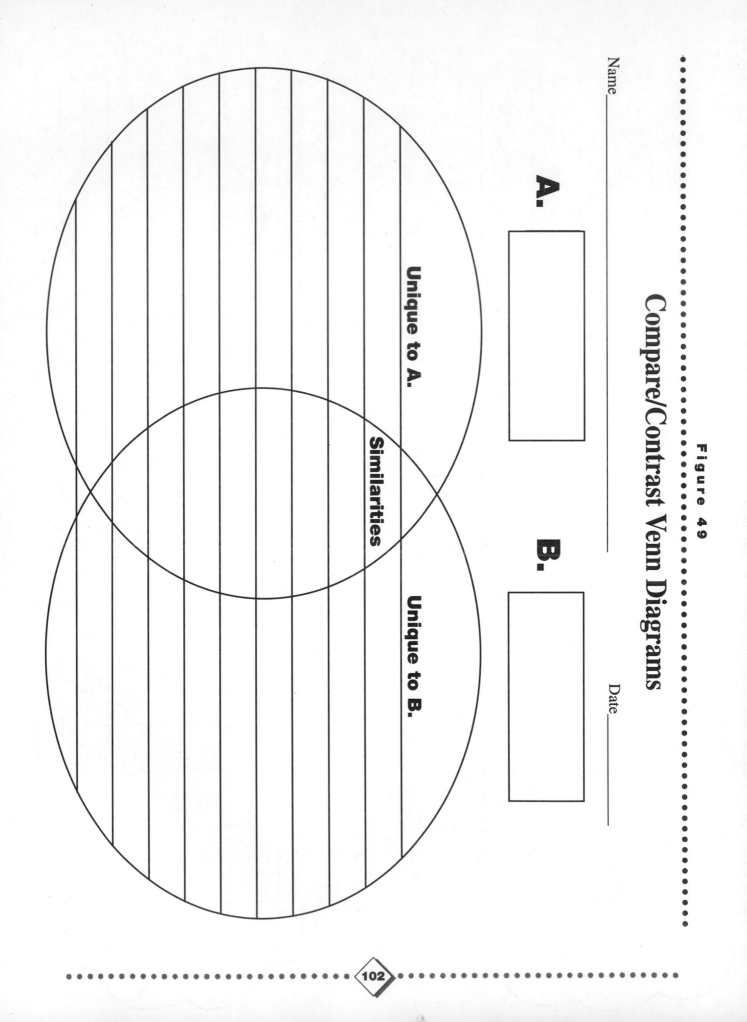

A. [ ]

B. [ ]

Unique to A.

Similarities

Unique to B.

Figure 50

Primary Organizer

Name_____   Date_____

Title of book_____   Author_____

What's On _____'s Mind?
the book's main character

What are the kinds of things your character thinks about? Write them inside the boxes.

What does your character think about each of these things? Write your answers on the lines.

Figure 51

Upper Elementary Organizer
My How You've Changed

My Name _____

What he or she was like at the beginning

The Main Character's Name _____

Book Title _____

What he or she was like at the end

Evidence

Possible Reasons for the Change

Evidence

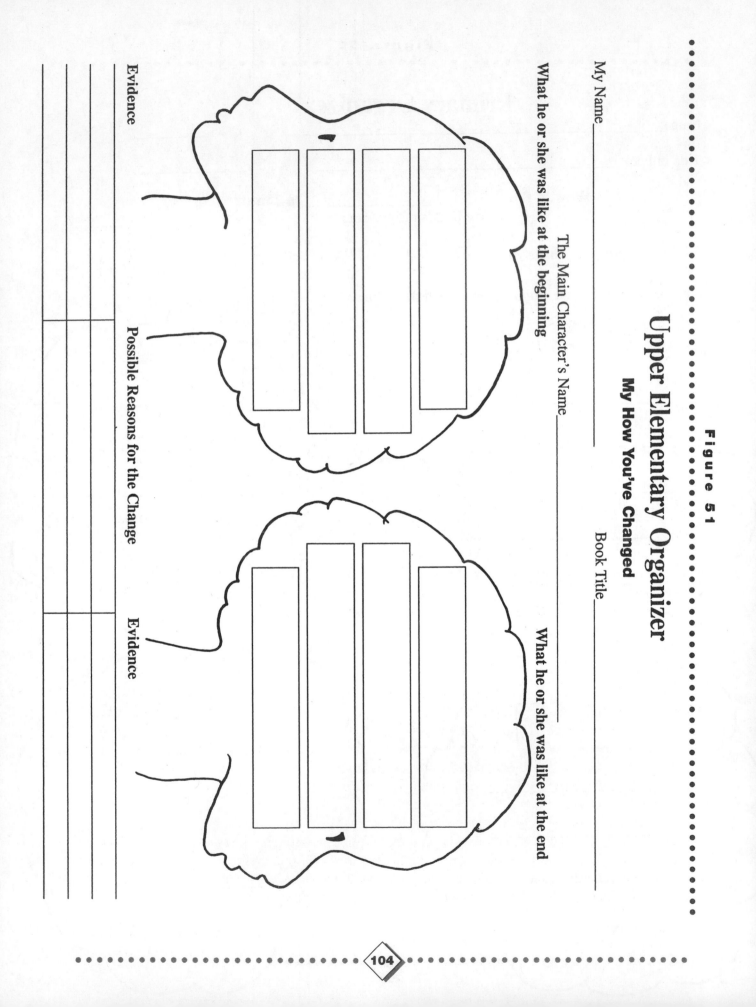

CHAPTER

6

Evaluating Learning Through Additional Reading Activities

Most teachers I know think long and hard about the activities their students will engage in during a 45- to 60-minute reading block. In addition to setting aside time for reading, they also have to decide which additional activities will foster reading growth and literary understandings best in their students. Although teachers' choices vary somewhat, most teachers believe that one-to-one reading conferences, literary discussions, and book projects are vital components of their reading programs. This chapter, therefore, extends the previous chapter with additional ideas that you can use for assessment and evaluation through daily reading activities.

TEACHER-STUDENT READING CONFERENCES

A conference usually will help you see what each student can do and cannot do—yet. It also offers you a convenient opportunity to follow-up an assessment with an appropriate mini-lesson. In other words, as soon as you discover something a child needs to learn, teach it! If you are like most teachers, you probably have discovered that independent reading time is the best time for your one-to-one reading conferences. Although the time you may spend with each child varies, meeting for several minutes with a student should enable you to have two or three conferences each day.

Because one-on-one conference time is so precious, it's important to use it as efficiently as possible by first deciding where you will meet with your students—at a conference table or at their desks. Then in advance, alert those students who will meet with you so that they can prepare any records or materials you want them to have on hand. Also, have your own supplies ready, such as your students' anecdotal records, an audiotape and recorder, and any forms you plan to use for recording miscues or taking running records. (You will find copies of these and other reading assessment forms in Chapters 2, 3, and 4.)

Conference Agendas

If you teach emergent or developing readers, you probably will want to spend most of your conference time listening to them read, but whatever your grade level, always leave some time to chat in a natural way about reading and books. One good way to begin a conference, for example, is to ask, "How's everything going?" Then take your lead from a child's response. You also could begin by saying something such as, "Oh, I see you're reading Patricia MacLachlan's new book. I just loved *Sarah Plain and Tall*. How's this one?" To end a conference, let the student know that you enjoyed the discussion. Then ask what the student's future plans are.

Teacher Observations during Conferences

Jotting down a few notes during a one-to-one conference is crucial for keeping track of what each student can do and what they need to learn. Following are just a few examples of important areas that most teachers focus on during such teacher-student conferences throughout the year. First, a word of advice: Don't try to cover too much in a single conference and do more listening than talking. (To review what you should look for and listen for during a conference, refer to the Reminder Lists on pages 40-41 [Figures 16a and 16b].) You also may want to refer to the suggestions made about reading conferences in Chapter 2 on pages 30-32.

What reading strategies do your students rely on? (Ask questions such as those on the Reading Strategy Survey forms on pages 43-45, [Figures 18a, 18b and 19].) It's a good idea to keep a chart of reading strategies developed by your class near the conference area so that you and your students can refer to it easily. See, for example, the chart entitled "Stuck on a Word?" on page 114 [Figure 54].

What meaning are your students getting from the story? To a particular student you could say something such as, "I see you're on page 32. Please tell me what's happened so far in the story so I'll be able to understand the part you'll be reading to me today."

How appropriate are the books your students select? Look at their booklists with your students. If the books are consistently too hard or too easy, suggest a way they can make better choices—such as the five-finger strategy described on page 30 in Chapter 2.

How involved are your students with a story? You could ask questions such as, "How do you feel about this book?" or "What made you think it was your kind of book when you chose it?

How thoughtful are your students' reading responses? Have them read the best entry in their reading notebooks. If your students' ideas need to be developed further, encourage them to tell you more about them. Suggest that they use a graphic organizer to generate their ideas before writing.

How involved are your students with reading in general? Find out what kinds of books or magazines they are reading in school and at home. Ask about their reading interests and look at their book records to discover the genres, authors, and series they prefer.

For examples of teachers' notes and a blank anecdotal record form that you can photocopy, see pages 37-39 [Figures 14a, 14b, and 14c].

Use of Audiotapes during Conferences

If you have already audiotaped your students' read-alouds early in the year, repeating the tapings periodically during your individual reading conference times will give you a basis for comparison and help you determine the individual progress your students have made. However, if you have not made any audiotapings, it's still not too late to begin. Even a single audiotape can be useful for analyzing a child's reading performance. (See, for example, the Miscue Record Form on page 57 [Figure 30] that was completed by a second grade teacher while listening to her students' audiotaped readings.) Many teachers also send home audiotapes as an excellent way of involving parents and children in reading assessments. (For ideas about how to make these assessments work, see pages 134-137 in Chapter 8, "Making Home-School Connections.")

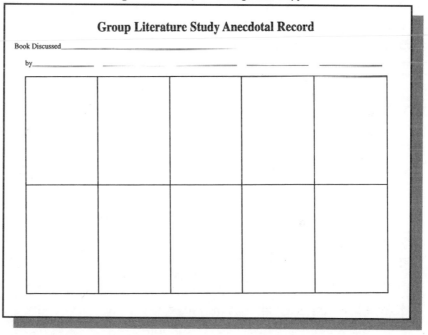

Figure 55: Example

Group Literature Study Anecdotal Record

Book Discussed *Charlotte's Web* by *E.B. White*

by *Todd*   *Mariko*   *Julie*

| 1/16 Identifies problem "Mr. Z. trying to kill Wilbur and eat him." | Describes characters in simple way "Templeton is dirty, not nice. Charlotte's nice. She tried to make Wilbur a friend." | Funny parts "When Charlotte and the goose and Wilbur talked." Described the buttermilk bath. | | |
| 1/23 Recognized solution: "Charlotte wrote words in the web about Wilbur— made him special." My question: "Everybody's got to die sometime." | "Charlotte is pretty nice. She helped him not die when she wrote 'some pig' and 'terrific'." What do you no response | "Pretty sad and pretty happy ending. Wilbur's saved but charlotte's dead." think E.B. White was trying to tell us in his ending? "Be nice to animals." | | |

Figure 56: Sample—Enlarge and Copy

Group Literature Study Anecdotal Record

Book Discussed_____

by_____

LITERARY DISCUSSIONS

"I didn't know what I was thinking until I heard myself say it out loud." You have probably heard or said something like that to yourself at one time or another. This phrase is just as true for children as it is for adults, according to Joan Tough, a researcher of children's spoken language. In fact, Tough believes that talk offers children even greater flexibility for expressing ideas than does writing or drawing. Whatever grade you teach, you will find that read-alouds provide wonderful opportunities for thoughtful discussions.

First grade teacher Mary Hayter, for example, introduces a book with a discussion of its cover and title. Then based on the clues provided in the illustrations, she asks her students to predict what the story might be about. She will also often ask her students to explain their predictions by drawing on their prior experiences with other books and events in their own lives. At different points in the story, she often pauses and asks, "What do you think is going to happen next?" and "What makes you think so?" After the story's conclusion, Mary invites her students to reflect on it by asking, "Any additional questions or comments?" or "Did anything surprise or puzzle you?"

One day during a discussion of *Harry Takes a Bath* by Harriet Zeifert, one of Mary's students responded to her question by asking, "Who was calling Harry to take a bath from upstairs? The picture doesn't show who it is." A vigorous debate followed that question as children offered a variety of opinions. One student, for example, said that it was the mother, but another student said, "No, maybe the mother works. If she does, it could have been the father or a babysitter."

I tried out Mary's strategy with my own fourth graders and discovered that the seemingly simple question "Any questions or comments?" was a great stimulant to their thinking. The great advantage of such informal literary discussions, I believe, is that they become models of thoughtful interactive response that my students can emulate when they meet with classmates to talk about books.

Discussion Groups

Discussion groups—such as book clubs, novel groups, or literature circles—allow students in groups of two to six to meet regularly and explore their ideas about a book. Depending on the readers' level of development and the teacher's preferences, these groups may be self-led or teacher-led. In my own third and fourth grade classrooms, I chose to form book clubs according to the selections children made from the books I provided—rather than by placing children with similar reading abilities together. The clubs were led by the students themselves while I rotated among the groups, joining in on some of their discussions. I also acted as an observer, making quick assessments of students' contributions (or lack thereof) and jotting down any perceptive comments I heard.

Teacher Observations during Literary Discussions

During literary discussions, I record information on sticky notes; later I place the notes on a page in each student's anecdotal records. Following are a few examples of my notations of children's comments.

Figure 58: Example

Dear Group,
I thought the book got alot better at the end and made you want to forget about the boring parts. I wonder why the author didn't make the whole book exiting. I think the reason our group picked this book was that the cover made you want to read the book. If you noticed the words on the front cover "The thing was ticking away, marking off the minuts untill domes day." I don't remember the author talking to much about domsday. I don't know why the author made the book boreing by putting in so many details. It would have been better if it made the book with Kevin's and Tenby looking for the clock.
I don't know what book we should read next but I know a more chalenging book
From
Katharine

◆ *I didn't like Viola Swamp because she's every child's nightmare and not the nicest substitute.*

◆ *I thought the cabin was pretty big, but it says in the book that it was small—one window by the bed, and some hooks on top of the door, like on top of where the gun was.*

◆ *This should win the Newbery Award because it's the funniest book I've ever read.*

Some teachers I know prefer to record their observations in their teacher's notebook or on a group record form affixed to a clipboard—such as the records shown above in figures 55 and 56. The only disadvantage, of course, is that the information involves several students, and you would have to make photocopies if you want to include the notes with each student's records.

How to Prepare for a Book Club Meeting

1. Read the pages you and your group assigned yourselves.

2. In your notebook or on sticky note page tabs, write at least two things you would like your group to discuss. Think about topics such as:

◆ something that puzzled you
◆ something that surprised you
◆ something that reminded you of something else
◆ something interesting that you noticed
◆ something special about the author's writing (quote the author's words)

Whatever system you use for recording your observations, it's a good idea to have a notebook, sticky notes, or a group record form handy when you join a literature study group. A word of advice: Never worry about trying to get everything down. With practice, you will learn how to become more selective in your recording. Also, don't miss the opportunity to share the information you record with your students in individual conferences or with the group. Whether you write their perceptive comments or simply note a strategy—such as "Jimmy made a prediction and gave reasons"—you will be giving your students a good idea of the criteria you value and look for in literary discussions. It's likely that such understandings will lead to more thoughtful responses even when your students work together on their own.

Self-Evaluation Processes

You may find that it's easier to keep track of what members of a discussion group are doing if you ask your students not only to monitor their preparation and participation in the group's discussions but also to evaluate their own meetings. For students to accomplish this goal, you will need to provide them with a literature study record form such as the one shown on pages 115-116 [Figures 57a and 57b].

If you want to get more information about a discussion than the form provides, ask your students to write to you about the day's discussion in their reading notebooks. These written assessments will let you know which groups are going well and which groups need your prompt support. For example, the following letter informed me that the Lizard Music group was doing fine and could continue to work independently.

My reading group is Lizard Music. We are on chapter 15 and there are 18 chapters in the book. I think D. Maunus Pinwater has a wild imagination. One of our most interesting conversations was Why does the Chicken Man have so many names? We never really figered out the answer. But now Victor is in Thunderbolt City. The book can only get more interesting.

On the other hand, the letter on page 110, written by a member of another group, alerted me to problems her group was having. After reading Katharine's letter, I knew I needed to participate in the group's next discussion—either to help the students make sense of the story or to suggest that they consider choosing a less challenging book.

We are reading a book called The House With the Clocks in its walls. We ushually talk about all the things that we don't understand in the story or what he's talking about. I think that the first 110 pages didn't make any sense to me.

Despite the difficulties Katharine and the others in her group were experiencing, they persevered to the end. In her final letter on page 108 [Figure 58], Katharine points out how the author could have improved the book.

STRATEGIES FOR THOUGHTFUL DISCUSSIONS

Just as with response writing, thoughtful discussions don't just happen; they need to be modeled during your read-aloud times and continuously nurtured throughout sharing sessions. Because I believe it's also important to offer students strategies for conducting their own discussions, I ask them to come to meetings prepared with written questions, issues, or ideas for their group to explore. Following is an example of strategies that you may want to adapt for your own students. Because they are designed to encourage explorative thinking, they do not call for single "correct" responses.

Discussion Questions

Good children's novels often present students with puzzling or surprising situations that have no easy solutions. For this reason, it was not difficult for my students to come up with the following discussion questions and issues.

◆ If Grandfather liked Willie and the potato farm so much, why did he want to die? (*Stone Fox*)

◆ What do you think Aslan said to the witch? It doesn't say on p. 140. (*The Lion, the Witch and the Wardrobe*)

◆ Chapter 3 page 23. It reminds me when I eat a chocolate bar and then when I eat an apple or something It tasts like chocholate. (*The Chocolate Touch*)

◆ Why was the title *Lizard Music* when the main point of the story is not about lizard music?

Discussion Guidelines

If your students are not used to managing their own book discussions, you probably will need to provide some guidance at the beginning. For example, they will need assurances that most good discussion questions have no easy answers and that only after they have thought about what they have read can they make a good guess. A word of advice: Encourage your students to refer to the text to support their ideas. You may even want them to outline your suggestions on a form such as the one on page 117 [Figure 59].)

When the members of a group complete their book, ask them to pull together the ideas they have developed and exchanged throughout all of their meetings. Then in a letter to you or to their group, they should summarize their reactions to the book they just completed. For example, in the letter she wrote to her group, Katharine criticizes the misleading blurb on the front cover of *The House with a Clock in Its Walls*. Then she suggests ways the author could have improved the book. (See page 109 [Figure 58].)

Alternative Group Formats

A good way to help younger readers and/or struggling readers manage their own discussions is to show them how to use the following four strategies that are borrowed from reading researchers Ann Palincsar and Ann Brown's "reciprocal teaching" ideas: summarizing, questioning, clarifying, and predicting. One significant difference between this approach and the literary discussions previously described is that children can read portions of the text to themselves or to each other during the group's meeting time. After a reading, however, the children should discuss the section of the story they have read or heard. Hearing parts of the story read aloud will help those children who don't read as well as others in the group to better understand a book that is a "reach" for them. (You may want to adapt the following guidelines, developed for third graders, for your students.)

Reading a Book with Friends

Everyone decides how much the group should read before stopping to discuss that part. Students can read as little or as much as they want, but the group decides whether everyone reads silently or takes turns reading aloud. After each reading, students should follow the guidelines below.

1. Summarize. Everyone talks about what they learned from the part they read or heard.

2. Question. Students ask questions about things that surprised them or that they didn't understand.

3. Clarify. Students try to answer other students' questions by making guesses. Then they find the part in the story that supports their guesses.

4. Predict. Students tell what they think might happen next.

Given the opportunity, groups of students often modify the discussion guidelines above and develop their own reading styles. One way to learn about their styles is to ask your students to write to you describing the way their group works and what they like about it. The following three responses—written by third graders— show that a variety of groupings is necessary to meet all students' preferences and needs.

◆ *When we are in a good interesting chapter we don't want to stop because it is too interesting. But at the end of it we do to find out what Misako leard [learned] and what I learnd [and] to see what her prodict [prediction] was and what my prodict was.*

◆ *My philosophy is to read the whole book then have a big long conference. On the other hand...if you don't understand a word or part, you can ask your partner. Like when I didn't understand what a woebegone little figure [was] Katie and I decided it meant a very sad pathetic little figure.*

◆ *When your Reading with a friend it's like a whole nother recess. You get to be with your freind and discuss the Book and if you have a partener and when you Don't understand something you can alwai's ask your Partener. and if your reading a hard Book you might want to read with somebody on a Higher Level in reading. I myself am a very good reader . . .*

PROJECTS

You are probably familiar with artistic projects as a way to help children respond to literature. Using a variety of art forms—such as drawings, models, cartoons, and murals, as well as through writing, drama, and dance—students can express and interpret important ideas they find in the books they read. However, the question most teachers have when they look at an artistic project is, "What does this show about what the student knows?"

Strategies for Planning Projects

One answer to this question is to have your students first organize their ideas visually by designing a planning web, map, or chart. If, for example, a group of students wants to dramatize a story, they could create a planning web for their play. If you teach upper elementary students, you may want to suggest the web in figure 60 (Page 113) to help them think about the characters and scenes they will include in their play.

Whatever strategies your students use to organize their ideas, remind them to include any diagrams or drafts they create with their projects so that you can assess not only the ideas that went into their planning but also their ability to develop an effective presentation of those ideas.

Projects across the Curriculum

Many teachers culminate content area readings and activities by asking their students to develop projects that show something important that they have learned. If your students work on projects independently or cooperatively, it's a good idea to have them include their research notes and a bibliography—as well as their planning organizer—with their project. Let them know in advance what you will look for when you read their research notes—for example, if the students organized their information into topics and subtopics and whether they paraphrased information by using their own words. (For examples of teacher-student evaluation forms for projects following an integrated reading-science study of whales and whaling by fifth graders, see pages 118-120 [Figures 61, 62a, and 62b].)

However your classroom project activities originate—whether through a literature study or an interdisciplinary unit—be sure to show your evaluation form before your students begin their projects. By sharing your criteria and expectations with them and by adding their ideas to your own, you will greatly increase your students' chances for success.

Before going on to the next chapter, you may want to refer once again to the Reading Curriculum and Assessment Planning Chart on page 89 [Figure 38b] because this is a good time to jot down any assessment strategies that you are already using as well as a few new ones that you would like to try out. As you begin experimenting, there are two essentials to keep in mind. First, always step back and ask yourself, "What's working well?" and "What's not working that I can adapt or eliminate?" Second—but equally as important—let no assessments diminish the delight that your students take in reading a good book!

Figure 60: Example

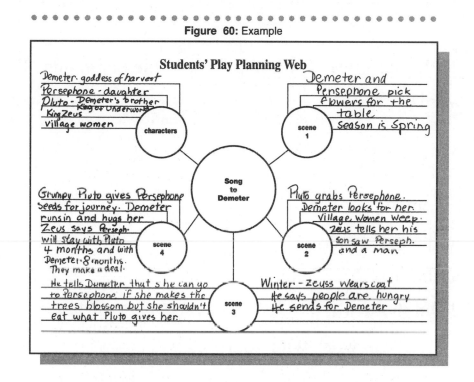

Figure 54

Stuck On A Word?

Think!!

1. Look at the pictures to help you.

2. Look at the sentence. Try going back to the beginning. Try going past the word.

3. Look at the word.

Sound it out.

Look at the first letter.

Look at the first three letters.

Slide down the word.

Cover part of the word with your finger.

Find the same word on another page of the book.

4. Ask a friend.

5. Ask the teacher to give you a hint.

6. Ask the teacher to tell you the word.

7. Look in the dictionary.

Compiled by First and Second Grade students, Bronxville Elementary School

My Group Literature Study Record

Name _____

Title _____

Date	Brought Book	Prepared For Discussion	Participated in Discussion

Comments

Date	Brought Book	Prepared For Discussion	Participated in Discussion

Comments

Date	Brought Book	Prepared For Discussion	Participated in Discussion

Comments

Date	Brought Book	Prepared For Discussion	Participated in Discussion

Comments

Date	Brought Book	Prepared For Discussion	Participated in Discussion

Comments

Date	Brought Book	Prepared For Discussion	Participated in Discussion

Comments

My Group Literature Study Record

Name _Lashawna H._ Title _The House with a Clock in the Walls._

Date	Brought Book	Prepared For Discussion	Participated in Discussion
5/6	✓	✓	✓+

Comments
I never thought about if there was a real place called New Zebedee. The group helped me understand the books more.

Date	Brought Book	Prepared For Discussion	Participated in Discussion
5/8		✓	✓-

Comments
5/8 The chapters I read were confusing. But the group helped me. The 1st meeting was better.

Date	Brought Book	Prepared For Discussion	Participated in Discussion
5/11	✓	✓	✓

Comments
The group didn't have very good questions but we made good discussions out of them.

Date	Brought Book	Prepared For Discussion	Participated in Discussion
5/15	✓		✓

Comments
James and I did not know the meaning of a word so we looked it up in the dictionary. I thought that was a good idea.

Date	Brought Book	Prepared For Discussion	Participated in Discussion
5/28	✓	✓-	✓-

Comments
I felt we did not do good because some people didn't have good questions.

Date	Brought Book	Prepared For Discussion	Participated in Discussion
6/4	✓	✓	✓

Comments
This meeting was the best.

Figure 59

Discussion Guidelines

1. Prepare your questions or ideas in advance of the discussion.

2. Everyone responds to each question or idea.

3. Ask new questions that come to mind during the discussion.

4. Everyone is entitled to an opinion.

5. Feel free to criticize or disagree, but give your reasons.

6. When there is disagreement, find support for your opinion in the book.

7. Everyone helps find support.

8. If there is time left:

Compare this book to others you have read.

Talk about how the book could be better.

Predict what will happen next.

Figure 61

Project Evaluation Form (Teacher)

An Evaluation of _____'s Project

on_____   Date_____
(topic)

1=Poor   **2**=Fair   **3**=Okay   **4**=Good   **5**=Excellent

1   2   3   4   5   **Interest and Creativity** (visually attractive, well-organized, teaches others in a creative way)

1   2   3   4   5   **Quality of Ideas** (includes important concepts and accurate information)

1   2   3   4   5   **Research Notes** (provides information in your own words, indicates quotes, notes organized according to subtopics)

1   2   3   4   5   **Bibliography** (indicates at least five references; follows conventional form: alphabetical order, underlined title, publisher, date)

1   2   3   4   5   **Presentation** (provided a clear explanation of the project, how it was created, reasons for selecting the topic)

1   2   3   4   5   **Participation** (if project was made by a group: shared work, contributed ideas and materials, listened to others)

Comments:_____

_____

_____

_____

Project Self-Evaluation (Student)

Name_____ Date_____

My project was a_____

_____

_____

I decided to make this project because_____

_____

_____

The hardest part about this project was_____

_____

_____

The thing I liked best about my finished project is_____

_____

_____

If I had more time, I would have_____

_____

_____

I think learning about my topic was _____

because_____

_____

Something else you should know is_____

_____

_____

Here's how I would rate my project:

_____

yucky   **just fair**   **okay**   **pretty good**   **great**

Self-Evaluation Of My Project On Blue Whales

Name Victor   Date June 14

My project was a blue whale magriting from polar to tropical whales

I decided to make this project because I knew I would have fun on it

The hardest part about this project was making the art work

The thing I liked best about my finished project is it's finished!

If I had more time, I would have add more details on my project

I think learning about my topic was interesting because the blue whale was the largest animal ever to exist and now I know about it

Something else you should know is that I had a hard time presenting to the class

Here's how I would rate my project:

yucky   just fair   okay   (pretty good)   great

CHAPTER

7

Showcasing Portfolios

*I*n the past few years teachers, individually and collaboratively, have begun experimenting with portfolios as an alternative approach to traditional testing and grading systems. Used in many different ways from kindergarten through college, portfolios are collections of the work students do over time in authentic classroom learning activities. Although portfolios usually contain work samples selected to show the best a student can do, they also may include "before and after" samples that reflect change and growth—as well as work products that are particularly meaningful to the student.

What makes a portfolio different from a traditional "best work" collection, however, are the following two important features. First, the selection process is ongoing rather than a one-time event. Second, students are at the center of the assessment process because they choose what goes into their portfolios, and they decide why the various pieces belong there. As a result, portfolios become excellent tools for improving learning. When students select and reflect on the contents of their portfolios, showing the portfolios becomes a natural bridge to the home—a wonderful way for children to show their parents what they have learned.

CONTENTS OF A PORTFOLIO

Portfolios usually display a student's best work in several subject areas. Although I discuss only a portfolio's reading components in this section, I believe a combined reading-writing portfolio works well because the various aspects of language arts are naturally connected to each other.

Initially, to help your students understand the concept of a portfolio, invite people you know who keep work portfolios to show them to your students, or you might prefer to tell your students that when people—such as architects, artists, and interior decorators—make up portfolios, they usually include the following kinds of items.

◆ a range of work samples that show the various kinds of work they do
◆ examples that show how they improved something—perhaps by including photographs of a room or house before and after they made changes in it
◆ written comments by others indicating their opinions of the person's work

Afterwards, tell your students that they will use portfolios to show you and their parents what they are learning about books and themselves as readers. Then ask for ideas about what might go into their own reading portfolios. A fourth grade class generated the following suggestions.

◆ worst and best reading notebook entries
◆ a book review
◆ a graphic organizer
◆ a photograph of a book project
◆ self-evaluations
◆ an audiotape of a read-aloud or a storytelling
◆ questions or ideas that stimulated good group discussions
◆ a reading test (a written response to a short story)
◆ a booklist
◆ a genre bar graph

After you point out which samples you want your students to include in their portfolios, suggest that they choose any additional items that appeal to them from the class's brain-stormed list. Then, to make the portfolios reflect their real world reading interests, ask your students to include an item that reveals the kinds of reading they choose to do at home—such as directions for assembling legos, a recipe, a club newsletter, or a page from a sports maga-zine or newspaper.

Snapshots of your students at work—such as when they are reading, writing notebook entries, creating projects, and/or dramatizing or discussing books—also make wonderful addi-tions to portfolios. It is helpful, therefore, to keep a camera handy throughout the year in order to capture your students' images as they engage in these and other reading activities. A word of advice: Make sure you get one or more pictures of everyone in your class!

When your students are ready to "house" their work samples, offer the following sugges-tions about the different kinds of containers that they might use to display the contents of their portfolios. Encourage them to add to these ideas and then to make their own choices.

◆ looseleaf three-ring binders
◆ a box of clear plastic page protectors
◆ photo albums
◆ "trapper-keeper" type notebooks with pocket folders
◆ expandable manila envelopes

Organizing the Contents

Showcasing portfolios takes time and planning because your students need to accomplish several important tasks such as the following list that helped my fourth graders organize their portfolios. Also remember that if portfolios are going to go home at report card time, you will need to have your students begin organizing their contents at least two weeks in advance.

HOW TO ORGANIZE YOUR PORTFOLIO

✦Update your reading records (booklists, genre charts).

✦Review your work.

✦Write a temporary table of contents.

✦Select your "best" work samples.

✦Write evaluation notes that tell what's good about the sample.

✦Discuss your self-evaluations with a classmate.

✦Discuss your selections and your future goals with me.

✦Recopy your evaluation notes, organize the materials, number the pages, and write a table of contents.

Evaluating the Contents

Once your students have updated their reading records and written a temporary table of contents, they will be ready to look for samples of their "best work" to include in their portfolios. You may want to suggest that they begin with a work sample for which they have already made an evaluation. If, for example, they have been using sticky notes to tab their best reading notebook entries, then this would be the best place to start. However, if they have evaluated their booklists and genre charts, guided by the questions on page 94 [Figure 43], then that would be a good starting place. As they begin, your students will need temporary construction paper folders to contain the samples and materials that they gather.

After your students select samples of their best work, have them jot down notes that explain what makes each of those samples good. You may find that self-evaluation surveys—such as those on pages 86 and 126-127 [Figures 52 and 63]—will help your students evaluate their reading. Afterwards tell them to clip their notes or survey forms to their work samples. Encourage your students to discuss their evaluations with a classmate and make any additions or changes based on ideas that grow out of such a conference.

STUDENT-TEACHER CONFERENCES

Once your students are close to completing their portfolios, post a "Portfolio Conference Sign-Up" sheet so that they can schedule a meeting with you when they are finished assembling the contents of their portfolios. These conferences will give your students additional opportunities for self-evaluation and for goal setting before they write their final self-evaluations.

Before any conferences actually begin, make sure you have enough copies of the Portfolio Conference Notes form so that you have one for each student. (See page 128 [Figure 64].) You should be able to manage these one-to-one conferences easily because your students will be completing their portfolio selections and peer conferences at different times.

Encouraging Reflective Thinking and Self-evaluation

During student-teacher conferences, your classroom usually will become a beehive of purposeful activity with some students updating their booklists and genre charts, while others are writing their self-evaluation notes. This period of activity frees you to move about your classroom and have mini-conferences with students as they make their selections. You also may find yourself making comments such as these.

◆ Oh, this looks interesting. What made you decide to choose it?

◆ I'm so glad you chose this notebook entry. I see that you quoted the author's words to show the description you liked.

◆ Your booklist shows you just loved Marshall's books at the beginning of the year and now just look at the kinds of books you're reading!

One way to begin your conferences is to ask your students what each record or work sample shows about them as readers. Because some may not always notice all that a sample reveals about their knowledge, you may need to point out additional strengths—as well as some areas they still need to work on. Be sure to ask your students to tell you what learning goals they have set for themselves based on what they have learned during the preparation of their portfolios and during their conference. You will want to refer to these notes in follow-up conferences with your students and with their parents when you meet with them. (The following notes, on page 25, are excerpted from a full page of notes I made during a conference with a good fourth grade reader.)

Record Sample: Booklist

With their portfolio discussions fresh in their minds, your students will be ready to revise and recopy their evaluations, assemble their portfolios, and make a table of contents. (See page 129 [Figure 65] for a sample of a table of contents of a fourth grader's portfolio.) Following are a few examples of my fourth graders' reading notebook self-evaluations.

◆ The letter that shows my best thinking about a book is dated 4/11. I chose this letter because it shows that I can find a characters feelings and find out why they feel that way by something that happened in the book. I wrote that Robin didn't like living with her dad because her father thought that girls can't do anything and I gave an example of what he did.

"For an example Robin and Jeff took tennis lessons. One day Robin asked Jeff if they could play each other Jeff said he couldn't. Robins father said it wouldn't be fair after all Robin's only a girl." Sarah, grade 4

◆ I wrote my best letter on Nov 5. I tell that I picked the book *the Silver Chair* by C. S. Lewis because I had one of the books in the series called the *Voyage of the Dawn Treder.*

Here is a quote from this letter "On the back of the book it had all the titels of the boos in [the] series and each had a littel book talk about each book. I liked the book talk they did for this book thats why I picked this book." Eric, grade 4

Portfolio Conference

Name___*Jo*_____   Date_____

Description of Sample	Student's Comments	Goal
Book List	"Reading more and harder books since Sept. I don't read Franklin Dixon's Hardy Boys as much now. I read books by different authors. The Last Laugh and Whipping Boy took a while to read."	"To try to read harder books -- funny books, biographies, infor. books, maybe short stories."

Since the evaluations for each sample are fairly brief, you may want your students to combine them by writing one long self-evaluation about all the portfolio samples, or you may prefer to give your students special cover sheets for individual samples—such as those shown on page 86 in Chapter 5.

PRIMARY PORTFOLIOS

First grade teacher, Lindy Vizyak suggests the following structure for actively involving even young children in assessment— models and demonstrations, sharing, minilessons, and conferences (The Reading Teacher, Volume 48, No. 4, pages 362-364).

Models and Demonstrations

To help your students understand what a portfolio is, create your own and share it with them. One way is to print your name and draw a scene from your favorite picture book on the cover of a manila folder. Inside the folder, place a drawing of your family, a momento, or a drawing of a place you've visited, and something that reflects a special interest or skill. Explain the significance of each entry as you show the children your portfolio's contents. Distribute blank manila folders for the children to start immediately after the demonstration. This first step instills an immediate sense of ownership toward the portfolio.

Sharing

Encourage the children to add to their portfolios' contents beginning with drawings and writings that reflect personal interests and graduallly including work samples that they think are "good." Set aside several times each week for children to share their selections and explain the reasoning behind each entry. Of course, early in the year, most youngsters won't say much more than "This story I wrote shows I like to play with trucks." To model the kind of thinking they need to develop, suggest additional plausible reasons for including the entry, such as, "I know that you love to write and often write at home. I also see that you have a title for your story."

As your students develop more discrimination, you may want to reduce your sharing sessions, from every day to every week.

Mini-lessons

Ongoing portfolio mini-lessons help children extend and explain the reasoning behind their selections. For example, you may want to point out the following reasons for selecting specific portfolio entries.

◆ Pieces that show effort (something that you worked on for a long time).

◆ Pieces that show growth or change over time (something that you have learned that you did not know how to do before).

◆ Pieces that reveal risk-taking (something that was new and hard for you to do).

◆ Pieces that show personal interest (something other than schoolwork that shows the kinds of things you like to do on your own).

Use part of your minilesson to develop classroom charts listing the ideas generated during the lesson. See, for example, the chart A Self-evaluation Checklist for Literature Responses (primary) on page 100.

Conferences

Twice a month, Lindy's students meet with her or an adult volunteer to discuss and select one or two pieces from assessment data and work samples that she collects for each child such as a running record, reading and writing conference notes, a survey, writing samples, or a response to a book. After making their selection, the children record the reasons for choosing the piece on a prepared form such as the following, attach it to the selection, and place it in their portfolios.

PORTFOLIO ENTRY FORM

Name_____ **Date**_____

I want to include this in my portfolio because

_____

_____

_____

Primary Showcase Portfolios

If you want your students to bring home a showcase portfolios at report card time, you will need to guide them. Begin by focusing on only one subject area at a time. some first grade students I know do the following tasks to evaluate their reading responses.

1. Look through your portfolio.
2. Find your three best writings or drawings that show what you can do as a reader.
3. Use post-its to rate them 1st, 2nd, and 3rd.
4. Talk to a friend about the reasons for your ratings.
5. Have a conference with me to pick the BEST one.
6. Write about what makes it good on an index card or Portfolio Entry Form.
7. Clip the card or Entry Form to the samples and put them in your portfolio.

Although involving your students in this way takes time, I believe the rewards make the time spent on portfolios worthwhile. To learn more about reading-writing portfolios in different classrooms, read *Portfolios in the Classroom,* by Joan Clemmons, Lois Laase, Donnalyn Cooper, Nancy Areglado, and Mary Dill (Scholastic Professional Books, 1993).

Figure 63

February/March Reading Self-Evaluation Survey
(Upper Elementary)

Name_____ Date_____

1. How have you changed as a reader since the beginning of the year?

_____

_____

_____

2. What genres have you tried this year?

_____

_____

_____

3. Which is your favorite genre?_____ Which are your favorite books in that genre?_____

_____

4. Which author do you think does the best writing in that genre?
_____How come?_____

_____

_____

5. How has your reading improved since the beginning of the year?

_____

_____

_____

6. What problems are you having with your reading?

_____

_____

_____

_____

Figure 63 Continued

February/March Reading Self-Evaluation Survey
(Upper Elementary)

7. Which is the best book project (writing, drawing, artwork, model, dramatization, etc.) that you've done so far this year?

_____

What makes it good?_____

_____

_____

8. Check the things you need to work on next.

_____ Writing more thoughtful responses to books in your log.

_____ Bringing interesting questions and issues to your book club meetings.

_____ Participating in book discussions.

_____ Reading a greater variety of genres.

_____ Spending more time reading.

_____ Reading more challenging books.

_____ Reading easier books.

_____ Trying to choose books that you will stick with.

_____ Abandoning books that you don't like.

_____ Keeping better records of your reading.

_____ _____(your idea)

_____ _____(your idea)

Figure 64

Portfolio Conference

Name_____   Date_____

Description of Sample	Student's Comments	Goal

Figure 65

Sample Table of Contents Grade 4

MY   PORTFOLIO

Table of Contents

Introduction

Book Records 1-4

Letters 5-7

Reading Genre Chart 8

Evaluation of Reading Progress . . 9

Spelling Progress 10-11

My Best Stories 12-13

Writing Genre Chart 14

Something About Me 15,16

CHAPTER

Making Home-School Connections

*T*hink for a moment about the ways you learned to read in school. If you are like most adults today, you probably will recall "round-robin" reading groups, graded basal readers, worksheets, and vocabulary and comprehension tests. Because it's likely that the memories of many of your students' parents are similar to your own, it's important to use every opportunity—such as your Open School Night presentation, parent letters, and parent-teacher conferences—to explain how and why you are teaching reading through real books. After parents understand this approach, their main concern usually remains the same: *How is my child doing?*

Although reporting individual progress is essential, you should take an extra step by bringing the parents into the actual assessment process itself. If you do, you will gain additional insights about your students as readers while their parents learn what to look and listen for when their children read. In the process, parents will become more knowledgeable evaluators of their children's work.

SURVEYS

It's never too early to open communication lines with parents. One of the best ways to start is by sending home a survey—such as the one on page 141 [Figure 66]—for parents and/or care-givers to complete. The information parents give you about your students can be invaluable, particularly at the beginning of a new school year when you don't know your students very well. Surveys also send important messages; they let parents know that you value their insights, and they provide a general idea of the behaviors and habits you value in readers. Interestingly enough, your surveys also may stimulate parents' observational skills. For example, if you ask parents to tell you what they observe when a child tries to figure out new words, they probably will listen more closely the next time their children read in order to answer your question.

HOME-SCHOOL BOOKS

Many primary teachers begin the year by having their students take home books to read with their families. Although teachers organize their home-school reading connections in a variety of ways, their main purposes are to help their students develop a reading habit and to involve families in the reading experience. Many teachers, however, have discovered an additional benefit—parents gain a better understanding of what and how their child is learning when reading real books. A sampling of ideas that teachers use to promote home-school connections includes the following.

◆ In a welcoming letter to her students and their parents at the start of school, a first grade teacher asks children to bring a book with them that they have enjoyed during the summer. She encourages parents to discuss the book with their children so that they will have ideas for their class book sharing session. After the children and their teacher talk about their books, they fill a bulletin board with illustrations of their favorite parts.

◆ Another teacher introduces her children to an easy, predictable book that they memorize during a shared reading session. Then she sends copies of the book home with a note to parents asking them to help the children find five individuals to listen to them "read" the stories they have memorized. The members of such a listening audience might include a parent, a brother or sister of any age, a friend, or even a stuffed animal! This "homework" is always a joyful experience for both the child and the family.

◆ Barb Jansz introduces her first-graders and their parents to a year-long family reading program by sending home a book, a reading record form, and a letter introducing her home-school book program. (You will find her reading record form on page 143 [Figure 67a] and an adaptation of this form that you can photocopy on page 144 [Figure 67b].) In the letter, she explains three different ways parents can engage their children in a reading experience: by reading *to* a child, reading *with* a child, and reading *by* a child. (For an example of a letter that I composed and a list of tips for parents, see pages 145-146 [Figures 68 and 69].)

◆ In my own school district, first grade teacher Barbara McMahon prepares a booklet of activities that can be used with any book during each child's home reading time. For example, she may ask children to illustrate a favorite part, write about that part, indicate their feelings about the book, name a friend who might like the book, list any new words they learned, or do other similar activities. After the children take a week to complete the reading and activities with the assistance of a parent or care-giver, they return the booklet with their parent's comments. Then once the teacher writes a response to the parent and another to the child, the booklet goes home again for another week.

A word of advice: As your students become better readers, they will read longer books. As a result, you need to alert parents that it may take three or four days for some children to complete a book. You also might want to suggest that children who are reading longer books should read several pages aloud and the rest to themselves. (For examples of children's reading activities and parent-teacher comments see pages 147-148 [Figures 70 and 71].)

Managing Home-School Reading

The most important thing you will need to establish a home-school book connection is a well stocked classroom library with books for a wide range of abilities. A book record form is important, too, because it provides evidence of a child's growth over time. If possible, also obtain large-size, sturdy self-lock plastic bags to protect the books on their journeys. In addition, you should establish some kind of check-out/check-in system that your students can manage on their own. Because an effective book management system such as the following takes time to assemble, you may need to ask a parent or upper elementary students for assistance.

Figure 72: Example

1. Paste a library pocket into each book.
2. On 3 X 5 index cards, print the book titles and place the cards into the library pockets.
3. On additional library pockets print each child's name or have them print their own.
4. Paste the children's library pockets onto a large sheet of sturdy chart paper.

Once the materials are prepared, the system works well. When children select a book to take home, they remove the title card from the book and place it in the pocket on the chart that has their name on it. When the book is returned, they remove the card from their pocket and file it in the book.

If you teach an upper grade, look for opportunities to build home-school reading connections that make your students feel they are part of a wider community of readers that exists beyond the classroom. You can, for example, bring family book talks into your classroom by inviting parents, grandparents, and even older siblings to share the literature they enjoyed reading when they were growing up. Your students may hear such visitors discuss some of their own favorites such as *Charlotte's Web* or the *Hardy Boys* series or they may be inspired to read an unfamiliar classic such as *Black Beauty* or *Heidi.* You also may want to encourage family members to share their memories of library visits, school reading experiences, and the stories their own parents told or read to them.

Organizing Parent-Student Reading Notebook Dialogs

Another way to connect your students to their parents through reading is to have them write to each other about a book a child has recently read. Although response notebook entries are usually unedited, you need to decide if for this particular purpose you want your students to write a first draft, revise, edit, and recopy their letters into their notebooks. Judy Grosz, a sixth grade teacher, provides the following directions to help her students follow this process.

◆ Use the correct letter writing form.

◆ Write a short summary of the plot of your book so that the reader will know what the story is about. Be sure to include the book title (underlined) and the author's name.

◆ Write your reactions to the book. Think about the characters, plot, theme, setting, the author's writing style, or any other ideas you have about the book. Look through your reading notebook to find your most thoughtful entries. Make this letter one of your best.

◆ Read your draft to a friend or classmate and discuss any information that you might add or delete. Make any changes that you need to improve your letter before correcting mechanical errors.

◆ Copy the letter onto a page in your reading notebook. Ask a parent (or family member) to read it and write back to you in your notebook. Parents don't need to read your book in order to comment on it.

Courtesy of Bill Ackerman, Fifth Grade Teacher, Osborn School

Of course, less formal approaches work well also. For example, just before Back-to-School Night, you could ask your students to write to their parents about a book they loved or one they are currently reading. Then during that evening, ask the parents to respond to their child's letter. A word of caution: Without your guidance, some parents will respond with the kinds of "teacher-like" comments and questions that they will recall from their own school days—comments such as those below.

"You didn't tell about. . . ."
"Describe the main character."
"How does this book compare to others you've read?"

To avoid demanding questions and critical comments—such as those above—it is important to advise parents to respond to their child's letter as one reader would to another—perhaps by answering a question posed by the children, describing their personal reactions to a book they have read recently, or mentioning their own reading preferences when they were in elementary school. It is also a good idea to reassure parents that a brief, friendly note is perfectly acceptable. To show parents an example of a reader-to-reader dialog, you may want to write your own or read aloud the one from Bill Ackerman's fifth grade class above.

AUDIOTAPE ASSESSMENTS

If you have not yet made any audiotapes of your students' read-alouds, you may want to skim through pages 33-34 in Chapter 2. However, it makes no difference whether or not you have taped your students reading aloud at an earlier time because it's never too late to begin involving parents in this activity.

Before sending home any audiotapes, you may want to help parents become better observers and evaluators by following the suggestions below.

••

◆ Send home examples of parents' comments from any of those described below or from your own classroom collection.

◆ Offer parents an after-school workshop on assessing read-alouds. Play a taped reading while everyone records their observations. Then discuss possible responses.

◆ Discuss audiotape assessments in your Open School Night presentation or during your parent-teacher conferences. Explain some things that parents should look for when listening to children read aloud.

◆ Ask parents to listen to their children read at home while they note their child's reading behaviors and strategies.

◆ Provide a list of behaviors and strategies parents can look for such as the following.

••

What to Listen for as Your Child Reads Aloud

◆ Do word substitutions make sense in the context of the story?

◆ Do word substitutions sound like the word in the text?

◆ Does your child try to correct errors?

◆ Does your child pay attention to punctuation?

◆ What kinds of words seem to give your child most trouble?

◆ Can your child pronounce a word without knowing its meaning?

◆ Does your child read smoothly or word by word?

◆ Does the child read with expression? Are there pauses in the right places? Do the words in a dialogue sound like the characters?

••

Encouraging Parents' Observations

There are many different ways to involve your student's parents in audiotape assessments. Second grade teacher Lila Berger, for example, sends each tape home with a copy of the book and the following brief note.

Dear Parents,

Enclosed is a tape of your youngster reading a book of his or her choice and a copy of the book. This tape will help you see how well your child can read aloud as well as areas that need improvement. Because your assessments are important to me, I would appreciate your writing any observations you make on a sheet of paper or on the back of my letter and return them to me by Friday, May 3rd.

Parents' responses to Lila's open-ended letter varied, but all of them showed that parents make significant discoveries. Two mothers, for example, commented on their children's abilities in the following letters.

Dear Mrs. Berger,
We thought Jamie did a great job. He is much improved since last Sept. He was good at figuring out words by using the sentence context. Jamie reads with impressive expression. He skipped a few words and added some. He could read hard words like "contraption" and missed short words like "dials."

The story Jamie picked had a boy in it who reminded me a little of Jamie (collector, not good at basketball). It was fun to hear him read.

....

Dear Mrs. Berger,
Kim was nervous at the beginning. If she's unsure of a word, she makes up a word rather than sounding it out. That word continues throughout the story. She usually reads to herself because her voice gets tired and loses expression. She had trouble with words she usually recognizes.
Kim always picks Step Into Reading books. She reads and feels comfortable with their format.

The letter from Kim's mother was useful for Lila's own assessments. It also indicated that Kim still needed additional support in choosing a greater variety of books. Although Lila had previously noted that Kim needed to use more strategies for figuring out words on her Miscue Record form (page 57 [Figure 30]), Kim's mother's observations reinforced her own.

Using Surveys for Audiotape Assessments

Some teachers prefer to send home surveys that call for a child's responses as well as the parents'. (For two examples, turn to pages 150-151 [Figures 74 and 75, and for two blank forms, see pages 152-153 [Figures 76a and 76b].) If you prefer this approach, you could write a letter—such as the following—to your students' parents.

Dear Parents,
I am writing to ask you to participate in a parent-child reading assessment activity that will give you an idea of how well your child can read aloud. I've enclosed a tape of your youngster reading several pages of a book as well as a copy of the book. In addition, you'll find two survey forms—one for you and one for your child.
Please listen to the recording with your child. As you do, notice what your child can do well and also any areas that you think could be improved. Afterward, ask your child the two questions on the survey form and write any responses he or she makes. Then write your own observations on the second sheet and return the survey forms to me by _____ .
Optional: If you have time, ask your child to read aloud several pages from his or her current book. Then ask questions 3 and 4 on the survey sheet.

Sincerely,

Although sending home just a single tape is a valuable experience, periodic audiotapings offer an even greater potential for helping parents see improvement in their children's reading. You probably will also find that, with practice, parents will get better at making assessments. They will also become more knowledgeable contributors to your own evaluation process.

PARENT-TEACHER CONFERENCES

As anyone who teaches already knows, a parent-teacher conference is one of the best ways to let parents know just how their children are doing. Most teachers prepare a folder of records and work samples in advance in order to make the most of this valuable opportunity. My students' folders contained the following materials.

◆ the student's booklist
◆ examples of entries from the student's response notebook
◆ the student's reading background and attitude survey
◆ any whole class comprehension "test"
◆ a cloze exercise
◆ an anecdotal record form
◆ a running record or miscue analysis form for developing readers

If you teach younger children, you also may want to include any reading inventories you have taken such as the following.

◆ a Reading Ladder (See page 46 [Figure 20].)
◆ an audiotaped read-aloud
◆ print concepts checklists (See pages 47-48 [Figures 22 and 23].)
◆ a letter identification inventory (See page 49 [Figure 24].)
◆ a developmental spelling inventory (See pages 50-51 [Figures 25 and 26].)
◆ a high-frequency bookwords inventory (See page 53 [Figure 28].)

You may also want to include a Running Record and Reading Inventory summary sheet that presents parents with a clear and concise picture of their child's progress over time. See, for example, the summary sheet on page 154 [Figure 77a] that was developed by primary teachers in the Bronxville Elementary Schools. You will also find a blank summary sheet on page 155 [Figure 77b].

Of course, you may not be able to discuss all of the materials you have prepared because conference times usually are limited and you need to leave time for parents to discuss their own concerns and questions. Nevertheless, you will find that even a few visual examples of a student's work will go a long way in helping parents understand what their children can do.

Using Reading Continuums

A reading continuum, which displays stages of reading development with descriptors or learning behaviors that illustrate each stage, is an excellent tool to have and use at a parent-teacher conference. Reading continuums are usually developed over time within a school district by teachers working together to better articulate to parents the benchmarks of learning that occur within and across the grades. The great advantage of these continuums is that they give teachers and parents a common language for talking about growth in reading.

Even if your school district has not yet developed a continuum of reading stages, you may want to use the continuums on pages 40-41 [Figures 16a and 16b] for your parent conferences. If you do, it's a good idea to customize them by writing dates next to the stages as children reach them and by adding a brief anecdotal comment about a child's reading at each of those points. You can do this by referring to the anecdotal notes you have made for each student and by reviewing their booklists. For example, to prepare the following Reading Progress Summary sheet for her spring conferences, a first grade teacher customized a reading continuum by adding comments about each child. (see page 139 [Figure 78]) If you want to learn more about reading continuums, read *Practical Aspects of Authentic Assessment: Putting the Pieces Together* by Bonnie Hill and Cynthia Ruptic (Christopher-Gordon, 1994).)

SHOWCASE PORTFOLIOS

As I discussed in the previous chapter, showcase portfolios are another good way to answer the question that parents so often ask, "How is my child doing?" I always introduce portfolios on Open School Night by showing parents examples of what they can expect to see in a portfolio such as notebook entries, booklists, and any other samples that reflect the activities that go on in my classroom. Once when several parents commented on how the portfolio's contents gave them a good picture of what their children would be learning in language arts throughout the year, I realized the unique potential portfolios have for communicating curriculum.

Inviting Parents to Participate

I also let parents know that they can become part of this important evaluation process by reviewing the portfolios with their children at each marking period.

When the portfolios are ready to go home, I always include the following letter that explains the kinds of questions parents should ask their children as they discuss each work sample.

. . . .

Dear Parent,

As March comes to a close, it's time to let you know once again how your child is doing in language arts. That's why I'm sending you an updated portfolio with current samples of your child's best work in reading and writing. As you already know, the selections were made by your child and discussed in a conference with me.

Please take ten minutes or so to look over the selections as your child explains what each sample shows. Following are some questions you might ask at that time.

* What does this tell me about you as a reader (or writer)?
* How has your work changed since the end of November?
* What do you think you need to work at harder now?

I think you will enjoy looking at the contents of the portfolio and hearing what your child has to say. Afterwards, however, I will appreciate your sharing your reactions with me on the tear-off form below or on a separate sheet of paper. We will continue to use the portfolios in the classroom until the end of the year.

Sincerely,

I reviewed my child's portfolio. Here are my reactions.

_____

_____

_____

_____

A Continuum Showing ___Ezra's___ 's
Reading Growth in Grade___1___

EMERGENT	**DEVELOPING**	**BEGINNING**	**EXPANDING**
Date:_____	Date:_9/93 11/93_	Date:_2/94_	Date:_6/94_
• Relies on memory to "read familiar and predictable books (word patterns).	• Relies on print and illustrations.	• Relies on print more than illustrations.	• Reads beginning chapter books.
• Pretends to read using picture clues.	• Reads predictable books.	• Reads early-reader books	• Reads a variety of materials and genres with guidance.
• Understands directionality of print (left-to-right, top-to-bottom).	• Can name most letters and sounds.	• Uses Phonetic clues.	• Uses multiple reading strategies.
• Joins in readings of familiar books.	• Beginning to use phonetic and context clues.	• Uses context (meaning) clues.	• Reads silently for 15-20 minutes.
• Knows some letter sounds and names.	• Attempts to self-correct.	• Uses sentence structure (sounds right) clues.	• Pays attention to basic punctuation and dialogue when reading aloud.
• Recognizes some words in context.	• Recognizes simple and familiar words.	• Recognizes names/words by sight	• Beginning to write reactions to stories independently.
• Relies on story patterns and pictures to predict outcomes.	• Remembers the important events of a familiar book.	• Reads silently for brief periods, but verbalizes when reading is difficult.	• Recognizes several authors and different types of books.
• Response to books through drawings and dramatizations with guidance.	• Draws and labels story characters and events with guidance.	• Demonstrates story understandings through discussions and art work.	• Considers story content for likes and dislikes.
• Chooses books as a free time activity.	• Predicts story events using context and picture clues.	• Writes limited reactions to stories with guidance.	• Recommends books to others.
	• Selects own books to read.	• Selects appropriate books independently.	

Anecdotal Notes: book titles, responses, strategies, etc.

9/93 Ezra relies on print, but reinforces his comprehension with illustrations. Uses all strategies (phon., meaning, struct.) but not with total accuracy. Seems hesitant to try a more difficult Beginning stage book. The Three Little Pigs.

11/93 Becoming more fluent. Also more confident about his reading. Willing to try more challenging books.

2/94 Can retell a story easily and synthesize a plot concisely. Book language often appears in his writing, e.g. "It all began — etc." Detailed writing about a book. Reading The Giving Tree (Expanding book.)

6/94 Fluent, involved reader, Chuckles over plot development. Also reads non-fiction, e.g. Magic School Bus. Started reading The Littles — a medium chapter book.

Courtesy of Ellen Anders, First grade Teacher, Heathcote School

Parents' responses to portfolios—such as the following—are almost uniformly positive; some even offer their own evaluations, and others comment on the goals their children have set for themselves.

◆ The portfolio is very interesting. Sarah seems to have a good idea as to where she is as a reader and writer. She hopes to improve her reading by choosing more "challenge" books and at least one book from each genre.

◆ We enjoyed going over James' portfolio. He agrees with us that his book record list could be longer and that he should also be reading a greater variety of books. We will encourage him to read more, choose different types of books and help him prepare additional book talks. Thanks for all your help.

◆ I was surprised and satisfied to see Hiroki's reading ability increased so rapidly. It was the first experience for him to read English books. I hope he will get the ability to express his thinking well.

◆ I got very surprised to see Felipe's development mainly in reading. His portfolio shows that besides being school work, reading has give him much pleasure. We perceived that reading could help him express his thoughts and ideas much better. Therefore, we are very happy and proud of his development.

REFLECTIONS ON EVALUATION AND ASSESSMENT

Over the last few years I have made some important, personal discoveries about assessment and evaluation. One was the realization that portfolios are well worth the time that my students and I have to spend on the process—continually selecting, conferring, adding new samples, and removing old ones to find their very best. Another realization was the valuable connection between self-evaluation and learning. With visions of what makes something good enough for a portfolio in their minds, my students usually managed to create something even better than they had had before. What's more, the process that engaged them in evaluating their own work never interfered with their love of reading as I had first feared it might. It had, instead, helped them grow as critical readers.

A third realization concerns the role of parents. To be honest, I never had opened up my evaluation process to parents as much as I have recently. By including parents in the process of evaluation, however, I gained partners who truly understand my reading and writing curriculum and share its goals. Using a common language, we can talk with each other and the students about their learning growth.

Finally, I realized that assessment is a grand learning experience. Reading and attending workshops and conferences helped me learn new strategies to try out in my classroom. There I was free to experiment—keeping those that worked best, while abandoning others that proved too time consuming or ineffective.

If you are wondering how you might begin your own explorations through the assessment process, you are already on your way. Just select a few ideas from this book and adapt them to fit your needs. Then read as much as you can and attend workshops to learn what others are doing. I wish you much success in the exciting and evolving journey ahead.

Figure 66

Parent Survey About Reading

Dear Parents,

Please take several minutes to help me learn more about your child as a reader by responding to the questions below.

Sincerely,

Child's Name:_____

Parent or Caregiver's Name_____

1. What impresses you about your child in this area? (strengths)

_____

_____

_____

_____

_____

_____

_____

_____

2. What do you think are the influences that contributed to these strengths?

_____

_____

_____

_____

_____

_____

_____

3. What concerns you about your child as a reader? (difficulties, needs)

_____

_____

_____

_____

_____

_____

_____

_____

Figure 66 Continued

Parent Survey About Reading

4. List or describe your child's reading interests.

_____

_____

_____

_____

_____

_____

_____

5. Which particular books and authors are your child's favorites? How can you tell?

_____

_____

_____

_____

_____

_____

_____

_____

6. In what everyday situations do you see your child read something? (other than books?)

_____

_____

_____

_____

_____

_____

7. In what ways do you and other family members share reading and books with your child?

_____

_____

_____

_____

_____

_____

_____

Home Reading Record

Name __Abby T.__   Grade __1ST__

Date	Title	✔Read to child	✔Read with child	✔Read by child	Comments	Parent Initials
9/27	Good-bye, Perky		✓	✓	learned some new words. Seems very eager to read these books.	BOT
9/30	Moon Story	✓	✓	✓		BOT
10/6	The Shop					
10/11	I like the Dad	helped us purchase			Me too! Home + school them!	BOT
10/12	Call 911			✓	☺ OK	BOT
10/14	STRIPES			✓	☺	BOT
10/20	MIRRORS		✓	✓		BOT
10/26	Pet Day			✓		BOT
11/2/93	The Magic Machine			✓	OK	BOT
11/5/93	The Whale			✓	I'm seeing some progress in her reading. The Whale is a very challenging book	BOT
11/7/93	LIGHT			✓	OK	
11/8/93	Sssh			✓	☺	BOT
11/19/93	Arthur's Pen Pal	✓	✓	✓	This book took a little longer but she read it all! Oh my! A very challenging book.	BOT
11/23/93	One Ballerina Two		✓	✓	☺	BOT
12/3/93	PAINTERS Bug Watching			✓ ✓		BOT
12/5/93	Across the Stream		✓	✓		BOT

Courtesy of Barb Jansz, First grade Teacher, Riverwood School Illinois

Home Reading Record Form

_____'s Home Reading Record in Grade _____

(child's name)   (teacher)

Title of Book	Parent/Teacher Comments	Read			Date	Parent Initials
		By Child	To Child	With Child		

Adapted from Highlight My Strengths by Leanna Trail, 1992

Figure 68

Letters to Parents About Home Reading

Dear Parents,

I have some exciting news to share with you. Today our class will begin a new home-reading program that I believe will help every child become a better reader. Each day the children will choose a classroom or library book to take home. They will also bring home the enclosed Home Reading Record form so that you can jot down some information about the book. I would appreciate any comments that you can add to help me learn more about your child as a reader.

Please remind your child to return the Home Reading Record and the book to school when they have finished reading it. (It may take a day or a week.) I look forward to working with you on this project. Send me a note if you have any questions and I'll be happy to respond.

Sincerely,

Dear Parents,

Our home-reading program appears to be working well. There are a few things you should know about various ways to make home reading a pleasant and productive activity. You may also be interested in knowing the kinds of things you can look for when your child reads. For these purposes, I have also enclosed an additional sheet "Tips to Help Your Child Become a Better Reader (And Love Books!)."

Sincerely,

Figure 69

Tips to Help Your Child Become a Better Reader (And Love Books!)

1. Set aside a special time for home reading every day. Try to avoid scheduling a time when your child would rather be doing something else.

2. Make reading time as pleasurable and comfortable as possible so that your child develops warm feelings for books and reading.

3. Notice when your child seems to tire. A book can always be finished the next day—or the day after that.

4. Try different ways of reading.

◆ Listen to a reading by your child and show the pleasure you take in hearing a good story.

◆ Read to your child when the youngster is not yet able to read a book that he or she loves.

◆ Read along with the child when a book is somewhat difficult.

◆ Encourage your child to read part of a book silently and tell you about it.

5. When your child comes to an exciting part, ask the youngster to guess what might happen next. Then check to see if the prediction was right.

6. When your child finishes reading, talk about the story and the illustrations. Tell each other the parts you liked and didn't like, or what the story reminded you of in your own lives.

7. When your child gets stuck on an unfamiliar word:

◆ Wait for a while so the child can think about it.

◆ Suggest that the child look at an illustration for a clue.

◆ Remind the child to look at the first letter, read the line again, and make a guess that makes sense.

8. Some things you can look and listen for when your child reads:

◆ Was the reading fluent or word-by-word?

◆ Does the child pay attention to punctuation?

◆ Do the errors make sense? (That shows the child understands the story.)

◆ Do the errors look like the word in the story?

◆ After an error, does the child self-correct or keep going?

Figure 70

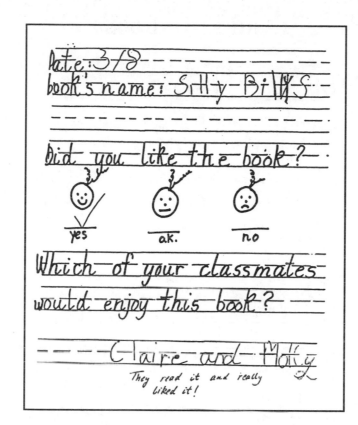

Date: 3/8

book's name: Silly Billys

Did you like the book?

yes   ak.   no

Which of your classmates would enjoy this book?

Claire and Molly

They read it and really liked it!

Draw a picture of a special part in the book

Write about your favorite part of the story. I likt the part about when the girl sasy, "you silly Billys."

short vowel i: Brg

long vowel o: So

short vowel o: chocolate

long vowel u: Xii

short vowel u: Cut

This book was:

easy   just right   hard

Figure 71

Examples of Parent and Teacher Comments

Comments from home:

Debra did very well with this book and words that
she didn't know she sounded out very well. good
Our routine is to read her book on routine!
monday nights, reread the book on Tuesday,
answer questions wed. + Thurs. This week
she brought home an additional 2 books
on Monday. Three books were too much
for her to read in one evening.
↳ from her reading program.

Teacher comments:

Debra needs to be reminded to use
word attack skills (th = one sound;
short + long vowels (& silent "e")) etc.
Also, I am encouraging her to
use context clues to help with difficult
words. She always scans the
pictures for clues!

Dear Debra,
   Silly Billy's is silly isn't it ?!
I am glad you liked it. The
more you read the easier it gets.

            Love,
            Mrs. McMahon

Figure 71 Continued

Examples of Parent and Teacher Comments

Examples of Parent and Teacher Comments

Comments from home:

Michael read aloud with much enthusiasm. He even re-read sections that he thought he had not read with enough expression. (I could hear you in the background!). I was surprised when he said he did not like it. But I think he only said this because he had read the book earlier.

Teacher comments:

The sentence structure in this story can be awkward reading. Yes! We are working on expression and punctuation. Self-correcting is a great accomplishment. Michael really enjoys the learning process.

Dear Michael,
You have heard this story many times. I've read it, on tape; now you read it yourself! That is a great thing! You must be very proud of yourself!

Love,
Mrs. McMahon

Figure 74

Example of Parent's Comments on Audiotape Survey

Please write any observations and reactions that you have after hearing the recordings of your child's two read-alouds.

What are your child's strengths? _Matthew reads very fluently and with good feeling and intonation. He enjoys reading and having books read to him._

What do you think your child needs to do to become an even better reader? _He is doing better observing punctuation and keeping his voice up. These improved_

Any other comments or observations? _He really enjoyed hearing the tape. It's good. Often time kids get to see themselves a great deal on the VCR, but don't get to simply listen! Matt was interested in recording and hearing his voice_

Courtesy of Valerie Rein, Second Grade Teacher, Heathcote School

Figure 75

Example of Child's Comments on Audiotape Survey

Child's name_ MATTHEW   Date 6/21

Title of book #1:_ The Teacher From the Black Lagoon

Question 1: What are some good things you noticed about your first read-aloud?

I could read words that I couldn't understand. I didn't make many mistakes. It felt good that I could read the book.

Question 2: What are some things that you think needed fixing up?

I mumbled a little bit. The tape made me sound funny.

Title of book #2:_ Mountains of Tibet   **Pages read** 5

Question 3: What was good about the way you read today?

It sounded clear. I stopped at periods and commas. I read with good style

Question 4: What do you think needs fixing up?

I don't think it needs fixing up. I had to re-read one or two words.

Audiotape Reading Survey (Child)

Child's name_____ Date_____

Title of book _____ Pages read:_____

Question 1: What are some good things you noticed about the way you read?

_____

_____

_____

_____

Question 2: What are some things that you think needed fixing up?

_____

_____

_____

_____

Now read a few pages aloud again. They may be the same that you read on the tape or different ones. Pages read_____

Question 3: What was good about the way you read today?

_____

_____

_____

_____

Question 4: What do you think needs fixing up?

_____

_____

_____

_____

Audiotape Reading Survey (Parent)

Child's name:_____ Parent's name:_____

Please write any observations and reactions that you have after hearing your child read aloud.

What are your child's strengths?_____
_____
_____
_____
_____
_____
_____
_____

What do you think your child needs to do to become an even better reader?
_____
_____
_____
_____
_____
_____
_____
_____

Any other comments or observations?_____
_____
_____
_____
_____
_____
_____
_____
_____

Running Record and Reading
Inventory Summary Sheet

Name **Doug**   Teacher **Heidi Menzel**   Grade **2**

Date	Title/Level	Accuracy	Comment
9/93	Grandma's Birthday Surprise (Primer level)	83% Required lots of assistance with sight words	oral retelling score 11/1 Needed assistance to retell
11/93	Word lists	Primer – 90% 1st gr. – 70% 2nd gr. – 45%	
11/93	Is it so? Six and six (Stern L-2)	Read 2 stories 85% Frustration Level	made many errors also many SC s able to piece story together for retelling
1/94	Rock Stew (level 2¹)	94% More fluent	Eager to express understanding sever. times during story
2/94	word lists	P – 95% 1 – 90% 2 – 75%	
2/94	Ant and the Grasshopper (level 2²)	96% 14/15 oral retelling	8/9 written compreh (to prompt) Read with confidence
6/94	Word Lists	P – 100% 1 – 95% 2 – 85% 3 – 85%	
6/94	Hattie the Backstage Bat (level 3¹)	85%	good use of self-correction concise retelling answered questions well

Courtesy of Heidi Menzel, Grade One Teacher, Bronxville Elementary School.

Running Record and Reading
Inventory Summary Sheet

Name_____Teacher_____Grade_____

Date	Title/Level	Accuracy	Comment

Courtesy of Heidi Menzel, Grade One Teacher, Bronxville Elementary School.

References

Atwell, Nancie. *In the Middle: Writing, Reading, and Learning with Adolescents.* NH: Heinemann, 1987.

Baskwill, Jane, and Paulette Whitman. *Evaluation: Whole Language, Whole Child.* NY: Scholastic, 1988.

Clay, Marie. *An Observational Survey of Early Literacy Achievement.* NH: Heinemann, 1993.

Clemmons, Joan et al. *Portfolios in the Classroom.* NY: Scholastic, 1993.

Farr, Roger, and Bruce Tone. *Portfolio and Performance Assessment.* NY: Harcourt Brace, 1994.

Glazer, Susan Mandel. *Reading Comprehension: Self-Monitoring Strategies to Develop Independent Readers.* NY: Scholastic, 1992.

Graves, Donald, and Bonnie Sunstein (Eds.). *Portfolio Portraits.* NH: Heinemann, 1988.

Johnson, Terry, and Daphne Louis. *Literacy through Literature.* NH: Heinemann, 1988.

Rosenblatt, Louise. *The Reader, the Text, the Poem.* Carbondale: Southern Illinois University Press, 1978.

Ruptic, Cynthia, and Bonnie Hill. *Practical Aspects of Authentic Assessment.* MA: Christopher Gordon, 1994.

Strickland, Dorothy and Denny Taylor. "Family Storybook: Implications for Children, Families, and Curriculum." In D. S. Strickland and L. M. Morrow (Eds.). *Emerging Literacy: Children Learn to Read and Write.* Newark DE: International Reading Association, 1989.

Wollman-Bonilla, Julie. *Response Journals: Inviting Students to Think and Write about Literature.* NY: Scholastic, 1994.

 **Notes**